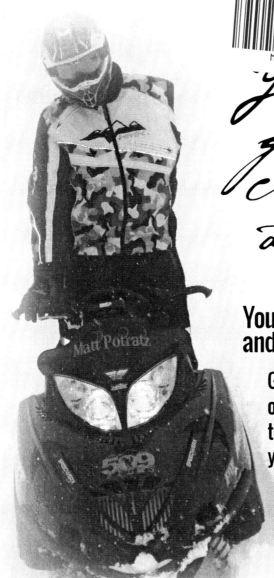

You only get one chance at life.

You cannot hit rewind and try again.

Get everything you can out of life by refusing to take anything with you when you leave it.

Don't stop giving until life forces you to.

It begins with igniting your *Passion.*
Find it. Fuel it. Follow it.

TWO HANDS

BY MATT POTRATZ

First Paperback Edition, designed by Firewind Productions and published by 212 Degrees, LLC in association with Firewind Productions; Lewiston, Idaho. For more information, visit FirewindProductions.com.

ISBN 978-0-615-52554-9 (First Paperback Edition)

Printed in the United States of America.

Dedicated to the three most amazing things that have ever happened in my life: **Connor, Ethan,** *and* **Caleb.**

May this book inspire you to walk in dad's footsteps. Use your TWO HANDS *to give, to hold, to love, to cheer, to shape, to design, to lead—to make a difference. Reach out and grab hold of life with both hands and touch your world... leave your mark!*

Thanks for giving me so many reasons to be the proudest dad on this planet!

I LOVE YOU!

"POTRATZ"

I think for all of us, our last name means something special. For me, it runs deep and is a significant part of who I am.

My full name is MATTHEW KURT POTRATZ. My dad's father, Kurt Potratz is as far back as I know, so that's where the Potratz name begins for me. From there forward, each generation gave him something to be proud of, including my three young Potratz boys today.

We've definitely made our mistakes along the way, but overall we love well, live well, care much, and give well. We work hard, play hard, invest our time wisely, and contribute to society in many ways.

During the publication of this book, my Grandpa Potratz left us to be with his Father in heaven. Minutes before he took his last breath, I sat by his bed holding his hand tight and looked at his weary face to say; "Grandpa, I want you to know how proud I am to be a Potratz. It's because of you."

"Most of your impact was without saying a word. We watched who you were and wanted to be just like you. I remember my brothers and I looking at the doors on your equipment where it said 'Potratz Logging Inc.' We were so proud that you were our Grandpa."

Breaking down in tears, I told him that my boys recently got little HMK jackets that say "Potratz" across the top on the back. "Grandpa, they are so proud to have that last name. It's because of you." Bursting into tears, I cried out, "Grandpa, I love you!"

He had responded very little all day but at that moment, he opened his eyes, looked at me and softly mumbled "I love you too." It was honestly the most powerful moment of my entire life!

I know that there are holes in the floor of heaven and you're watching us continue on with your last name.

Grandpa, you left your mark. You will never be forgotten. *This book is for you; to carry on your legacy.*

Acknowledgements

When we stumble in life and lose our footing, the rest of the world still walks on.

Friends like you hung back and carried me until I could crawl, crawled with me until I could walk, and today you walk with me until I can run again.

Thank you for YOU!

Ground Zero

Dan Bieker	Jason Caldwell	Phil Yribar
Tim Bieker	Jeremy Kinzer	
Chris Brannan	Corey Wonderlich	

Rescue Crew

McCall Fire and Rescue

Freddie Van Mittendorp, Captain AEMS-A

Lifeflight 74 Crew: Ontario, Oregon

Lifeflight 75 Crew: McCall, Idaho

St. Alphonsus Regional Medical Center Trauma, ICU, and Rehab & Recovery Staff

St. Luke's Rehabilitation Institute

Peak Performance Physical Therapy: Tami Biery, PT and David Biery

Dr. David Petersen, MD

Dr. Craig Flinders, MD, DABA, DABPM

Dr. Michael Ludwig, MD

Tony Edmison, PTA

Renee: Pacific Med

Brachial Plexius Team: Mayo Clinic of Rochester, MN

Family

Dad	Jessica	Jon
Mom	Chris	Joey

Friends (alphabetical order)

Roger Baker

Steve Barham

Travis Beller

Brad Bramlet

Aaron Bren

Rod Bond

Chris Burandt

Twila Bieker

Dan Culver

Austin Cunningham

Tom Delanoy

Mary Egeland and
 Family

Lee Fraser

Kayla George

Justin Greene

Jason Hackwith

Jeremy and Megan
 Hedrick

Joni Hedrick

John and Annette
 Heston

Amber Holt

Travis Hunt

Dave James

Jarrod Mangum

Cody Monroe

Doug LaMunyan

Debbie Moser

JW and Jennifer
 Nightingale

Mark Messenbrink

Cody Monroe

Rod Mykelbust

Sarah Potratz

Jason Pujol

Rich Rogers

Ryan and Wendy
 Rogers

Roger's Toyota®-Scion®
 Staff

Ray and Cheryl
 Schoenfelder

Ryan Skinner

Marty Wieters

Kirk Zack

Table of Contents

Foreword *by Doug LaMunyan*

I moved to the small town of Pierce, Idaho and began teaching all science classes at Timberline High School in the fall of 1996. I was a first year teacher; but not as young as some, having served in the military right out of high school for a little over two years. Matt Potratz was a big, tall, loveable sophomore with little knowledge about his potential as an athlete, student, or individual. Matt was one of my students in Biology, Chemistry and Physics for the following three years. I also coached him in basketball during that time as well.

I operated my basketball program like a drill sergeant runs basic training. Each year I broke my players down physically through stressful drills and high expectations. My hope was that the players would bond during the stressful time and as the season progressed. Although not always successful, my motivation was to build them up as a team so they would enjoy more success on the court. I felt as their coach that if a player could survive my program, they would learn the principles of discipline, persistence, and loyalty that would help them throughout their lives.

Matt was an excellent athlete and played with intensity, even with a hot temper at times. It took quite a bit to get Matt angry, but when he was angry he channeled that energy and became terror on the floor; grabbing rebounds and playing harder. I felt that Matt was a more intense player when he played angry, but at times it cost him his intelligence and decision making—as we can all be subject to when our emotions run high. I can attest that I likely cost our team many games as well; I too needed to learn to control my temper. Over the years, I've learned the reward found in learning to control my emotions.

Some experiences as a coach will hang on in my mind for life. I remember one practice when I felt that we were not playing physical enough on the boards. I borrowed a rebound drill that was inspired by George Raveling, an excellent coach who coached at Washington State University and later on at University of Southern California. Basically, the drill has three players trying to rebound a missed shot and put it back in the basket. One of the three would successfully grab the rebound then the other two became defenders as the rebounder attempted to battle the ball up for a basket.

Sounds pretty simple, right? The problem is that the player must successfully make three baskets in order to get out of the drill and rotate a fresh player in. As there are no fouls called, it is a non-stop, full contact drill. I always joked that the only thing illegal in this drill is murder.

Matt rotated into the drill and grabbed many rebounds, but was having trouble putting the ball back into the basket. Matt became more and more frustrated as he missed many easy put-backs; he fought through his teammates' contact for a miss about nine or ten times.

The intensity and frustration welled up, and Matt went ballistic. He got so mad that he ran up to the padded concrete wall under the basket, and head butted it so hard that it dropped him like a sack of dirt. The emotions of the team went from complete silence and shock to gut-rolling laughter as Matt rolled over and showed that he was all right. The team continued drilling while I took Matt aside and chatted with him about his actions.

Quite honestly, at no time was I disappointed with his emotion and intensity. Some coaches may not approve of that behavior and I don't necessarily recommend it, but I looked deeper and I love the fact that it meant so much to Matt. Matt played for me emotional, determined, full of desire to win and was in the process of learning how to direct his emotional energy.

His teammates voted for him to be recognized as "Most Inspirational Player" in an awards banquet at the end of a season. Matt and I spoke often about how to direct that emotion into effort for success, not effort to lose your cool or even inflict pain upon yourself—such as head butting a wall.

Sometimes it takes a traumatic and tragic event for us to get back to the basics of life and who we are.

Matt's leadership potential grew during those three years. He became our Team Captain during his senior year, on a good team that finished tied for first in our division. He was also voted into the position of Student Body President that year and graduated as an honor student and class Salutatorian. However, I don't believe that Matt really achieved his athletic potential until later in life when he became a professional snowmobile rider.

Matt and I lost touch for quite some time. I had heard that he was working at Rogers Toyota® when he sold my dad a truck. Dad heard about Matt's accident and passed the news on to me. I didn't realize how severe the accident was until Matt asked me to participate in a speaking engagement he had in Colfax, Washington.

Our audience was a group of young athletes attending a high school basketball camp. Matt decided he would like his own high school coach to introduce him before the presentation. I was honored with his request. We were able to reconnect and catch up on all that had happened since we last talked. It was rewarding to see the man that Matt had become, and the strong character traits he had developed.

So many times, we get so caught up in living life that we forget who we are as a person. We allow our job to define who we are, instead of focusing on being the person we should be. The youth of today often get their identity defined by the group that they hang out with, instead of being who they are within the group. Sometimes it takes a traumatic and tragic event for us to see this and get back to the basics of life and who we are. Matt delivered an emotional and powerful message that evening in Colfax; one that has made me reflect upon my life, and will make you reflect upon yours.

One of the biggest compliments and privileges of my career as an educator and coach was to be asked to write this for Matt. When I received the call, I was quite surprised, but deeply honored. Matt went on to explain that few, if any, had impacted his life to the depth that I had. I discovered that the lessons learned on the basketball floor and in the classroom carried much more significance than I realized. Those lessons helped him to develop the discipline needed to achieve his elite level as a rider, but also to be able to cope with the significant injuries he sustained—and the long fight to get back on his feet.

I am very grateful to have Matt back in my life, and you will be as well, as you read this book. There is no doubt in my mind that you will be changed by his heartfelt and powerful message.

Doug LaMunyan

– 1 –

LIFE HAPPENED

"We cannot control what happens to us. However, we can control 'what happens' to what happens to us."

David Foster

O N THE AFTERNOON OF MARCH 1ST, 2009, *LIFE HAPPENED.* My day started out as another average winter weekend morning, as I prepared to go share my passion riding the rugged Idaho backcountry on my snowmobile. For about four years, I had spent my weekends riding snowmobiles professionally for a couple of different film companies that produced highlight films showcasing backcountry riding each season.

On this particular Sunday afternoon, I was riding in the McCall, Idaho backcountry with 208 Film Productions out of McCall for an appearance in my sixth snowmobile film. We were all excited, as a couple of feet of fresh Idaho powder snow had fallen during the week, and the forecast called for decent weather. My television stayed frozen on The Weather Channel®—itching to see more winter storms on their way to dump more "pow," as we called it. The energy was positive and fun, yet intense as we loaded our gear bags in the truck.

Today, we all piled in my good friend Tim's truck with all of our machines in tow inside his twenty seven foot long, enclosed snowmobile trailer. We always had the right music mix for the road trip to help us get pumped up and inspired, but this time with a couple of new guys in the group, there was more visiting and laughter on the three hour road trip from the valley to the snow.

When the doors flew open at the trailhead, the positive energy spilled out of the truck. It felt as if we were set for a great day on the snow. There is nothing as sweet as the smell of the exhaust of freshly burned, 115 octane race fuel. As usual, at the trailhead we conducted a "gear check" for avalanche beacons, shovels, probes, and any necessary survival gear. Everything appeared to be unfolding as just another routine morning before hitting the snow.

Something was different, though. When I stepped out of the house at 6 a.m. to start the road trip from my hometown of Lewiston, Idaho to McCall, my girlfriend Mary crawled out of bed to stop me on the porch for a "be careful" kiss—something she had never done before. I got the crew rounded up and off we went from the valley to find the snow.

We had just passed through New Meadows, Idaho, and were almost to our destination when my cell phone rang. It was Mary. She hadn't been able to go back to sleep.

"Matt, I don't know why, but I just have a bad feeling. *Please be careful."*

"Babe," I said in a reassuring voice, "Don't worry. We won't push it too hard. I know I have three boys that call me daddy and hero, and you and a lot of people counting on me to come home safe. We'll stay off the big stuff and play in the trees today, I promise."

The day started out with great snow playing our way up from the New Meadows parking lot toward Goose Lake. My rear suspension was giving me some headache as something was malfunctioning and causing my track to skip on the drivers under the torque of the 250+ horsepower cranked out by my turbo-charged Arctic Cat M1000.

We continued to play in the trees and small slopes in the deep powder. The last memory I have of that day is when we had parked on a small ridge-top with the sun breaking through the clouds. The group was having a snack while Tim and I attempted to repair my suspension problem. From there, the group tells me that we continued on up the edge of Goose Lake and eventually over the ridge and into the Twin Lakes area.

My Last Ascent

In many places throughout the mountains in which we ride, there are steep, narrow, technical rock outcroppings that hold enough snow to make chutes that are often just a little wider than a snowmobile. One of our favorite things to do was what we refer to as "chute climbing." We would take our powerful machines quickly up these steep rock faces, maneuvering them up through the chutes with little or no room for error. If you ride snowmobiles in the mountains, you know exactly what I'm referring to. It takes being a bit daring, of course—but mostly experience and skill to successfully climb them without damaging body or machine.

The Twin Lakes area is home to the most technical chutes in the McCall area, a lineup that we called the "Upper Twin Chutes." We worked our way up to see how the snow looked. The group said that I did my second "slab check" of the day. This is something I would do on pretty much every ride into big terrain. I would simply find a small steep face and ride my snowmobile in a hard cut horizontally across the face to check the behavior of the snow. If it broke off in slabs, I would expect that a large hill could slab the same way, potentially causing a large avalanche. I would then avoid large, steep slopes that lacked trees or rocks to hold the snow in place. This second slab test again showed no signs of instability.

We had also climbed a handful of slopes that morning with no indication of slides. The first of three chutes in the lineup is not as steep or technical, so I made a run up and over the top without any problems. Then I prepared for the upper chute, which is quite technical and narrow. My brother Jon had lost his machine at the top of this one two years prior in the film "Vertical Ascent." Jon slid rapidly down the chute on his back, kicking himself off the rocks, narrowly avoiding injury beyond minor bumps and bruises.

The following year I stuck it right in the center of the chute half way up. I was riding with Jon that day, leaving him as one of the crew that climbed down in the chute to help dig me out and safely turn me around.

"Man, you just had to make me come back in this thing, huh?" Jon teased. We laughed. Even though I had successfully climbed it a handful of times, it was always a little intimidating.

Phil Yribar, the camera operator and owner of 208 Productions, set up to film the climb. With camera ready, I lined up to climb it. But (the group tells me), I then turned around and rode back to the camera.

"Not today guys," I said. "It just doesn't feel right. We should stay off this big stuff. Let's work our way to the Brundage side where there's more trees and rocks. It never slides over there." I probably made that move mostly because of the promise I made to Mary.

So, we rounded up the group and headed for the Brundage Reservoir side of the mountains. As I had mentioned to the guys, this area is littered with trees and rocks with a lot less wide open space. We rarely saw slides on this side. In fact, in the first area we stopped to play (Duck Lake, also known as Box Canyon), I had never seen a large slide. After playing a little, I told Phil that I was going to climb Box Canyon's only chute if he wanted to film it. This was a chute I had been up a dozen or more times. I was confident my machine would crest over the top even in the deep powder snow conditions.

Phil got the camera rolling and off I went. It appeared that there would be no problems. I was packing plenty of speed and roared toward the top of the chute. On this hill, when you broke out of the chute, you had to keep the machine on one ski in what snowmobilers call a "side-hill" maneuver across a relatively small open face before breaking over the top. A little bit technical, but still a routine move. This time however, the mountain had a different idea. I wouldn't go over the top.

When I crested out of the chute, it was wind-loaded and got deeper quite quick. I began to side-hill, even kicking a leg a little to propel myself, something I often did. It looked as if I would claw my way over the top—but then the mountain clawed back. It quickly became apparent why Mary had felt the way she did. Twenty-five yards above me, the snow fractured, breaking off the entire face in a three foot deep slab.

When I look back at the movie footage, I can see that I stayed on the throttle attempting to push through, but it was too deep and quickly became enough snow to consume myself and machine. I tumbled down the rugged mountainside, got separated from my snowmobile, and bounced off a small wall of rock—gaining momentum as the avalanche speed increased.

> *The force of the snow and debris slid the chinstrap from my helmet up my chin and face, bruising my cheeks and nose, and ripped my helmet off my head.*

Then, something strange happened. As I was sliding down the hill feet first, the force of the snow and debris slid the chinstrap from my helmet up my chin and face, bruising my cheeks and nose, and ripped my helmet off my head.

The trees on the hill—the very trees that we hoped would make it a safer area and help reduce the avalanche risk—then became my worst enemy. The punishing force of the avalanche carried me violently toward a large tree, more than two feet in diameter at the stump. It slammed me into the tree, bounced me off like a rag doll further down the hill, and buried me under the snow.

Man Down!

Reality set in fast. There was a reason why we strapped those beacons on before every ride and did our gear check. Backcountry riders can have a tendency to think we're somewhat invincible. It's easy to be aware that avalanches happen and that people do get caught, yet still feel confident that "it won't happen to me." *It had just happened to me!* We had some training, but no one in our crew had ever had to use the equipment in a real-life situation. Now the training would be put to the test with a life at stake: my life!

Immediately following the avalanche the weather added insult to injury by deciding that it was going to replenish the snow that had slid off the mountain.

The wind suddenly increased, and it started snowing hard. The group spread out, switched their avalanche beacons from "transmit" to "search" mode—which left only my beacon in transmit mode—and started searching frantically.

Following the guidance of the beacon, my friend Corey alerted the group. "Hey! I think I see his hand!" It was part of my hand sticking out. In less than five minutes I was located and unburied! When they uncovered me, they discovered the avalanche had planted me face down in the snow.

As an instinct the group knew that my face needed to be exposed to air if I was going to have any chance at breathing. They then made the executive decision to stabilize my head and neck and then roll me over as quickly and gently as they could. When they did so, they found my ears, nose and mouth packed with snow. Though I had been dug out very quickly, the trauma from the slide left me badly injured and unconscious. I was breathing, but barely. They were careful not to move me as they were unsure of the extent of my injuries, so they dug the snow out around me to affect my position as little as possible.

It was time to call for help. Part of the group headed for the ridge top to use a cell phone to call for a rescue helicopter. Calls and texts also went out to my brother and dad to let them know that what we dreaded, had happened—to spread the word to close family and friends. And, *pray!*

McCall LifeFlight 75 had already been dispatched on another emergency. Valley County dispatch then turned to LifeFlight 74 out of Ontario, Oregon. From the

> *They quickly realized that the storm had settled in, making it impossible to fly directly to the lakebed near the avalanche site.*

moment they hit the sky, they battled the same snowy weather we were fighting on the mountain. As they closed in on our location, they quickly realized that the storm had settled in, making it impossible to fly directly to the lakebed near the avalanche site. They were forced to delay the mission and head to the McCall airport, hoping for the skies to clear. A local ground crew had been dispatched as well, so the new plan was to use a rescue sled towed behind a snowmobile to start the rescue mission while they attempted to get the helicopter as close as possible.

The deep new snow made it difficult to get the sled up to our location. In fact, Tim had to use his machine with more power and a longer track to get the sled up the last hill. The group was elated to see the rescue crew. They had now been watching their friend unresponsive and wheezing for over an hour since digging me out.

The rescue crew did their best to stabilize me, secured me in the rescue sled and headed for Brundage Ski Resort where they hoped to land the chopper. It continued to snow steadily as they battled to get me out of the rugged back-country. The steady snow also continued to keep the helicopter out of the sky. They made another attempt to fly to the ski resort and again, got rejected by the storm. An ambulance was then dispatched to transport me from Brundage down to the airport. The snowfall broke just as they loaded me in the helicopter. Three hours from the call for help, they had finally won the battle and lifted off in route to St. Alphonsus Medical Center in Boise, the capital city of Idaho.

When they unloaded me and set my stretcher down on the pad, what they had all feared happened; I stopped breathing. Their hearts stopped pounding when they were able to quickly resuscitate me and my chest cavity returned to its slow motion. Upon arrival in the emergency room, the trauma team discovered that there were multiple severe injuries to be concerned about. The rough ride through the rocks and trees had inflicted massive trauma to nearly my entire body: significant head and facial trauma most likely resulting in traumatic brain injury, possible fracture of the cervical spine, broken ribs, a collapsed lung and a compound fracture of the left femur. Later, they would find severe left arm nerve damage at the spinal cord. These injuries, combined with asphyxia, put my body into a state of coma. Calls, texts, and e-mails began to go out with one message: *pray!*

My mom traveled the nearly eight hour drive to the hospital in tears. Her son lay on the brink of death. Numbly, she waded through some powerful and difficult thoughts. As she began to realize that she may be losing her oldest son, she made the choice to give it to God. She chose to give not only the situation to God, but to literally give her son to Him.

> *As she began to realize that she may be losing her oldest son, she made the choice to give it to God.*

As she drove, she reflected on the story of Abraham and Isaac in the Bible. Abraham offered his son to God, but God gave Isaac back to him. God was testing him to see if his obedience and surrender to God was greater than his love for Isaac. She looks back to say:

> *"I decided right then in my truck as I drove down the road with tears flowing down my cheeks that I would totally give Matt to God. I would trust that if He chose to take Matt, He had a plan to use his death to bring life and salvation to others. If He chose to let him live, that it would bring glory to God and peoples' lives would be changed as a result."*

Even so, she was not prepared for what she would see when she walked into the Intensive Care Unit room. She was crushed to see her own son with tubes, wires and hoses attached on every side of my body—including the tube hooked to the machine that was breathing for me.

Doctors initially reported that they were unsure whether to even treat my injuries, as it appeared that I probably wouldn't live through the night. If they detached the machines, I would simply be gone. *This just may have been Matt's last ride.*

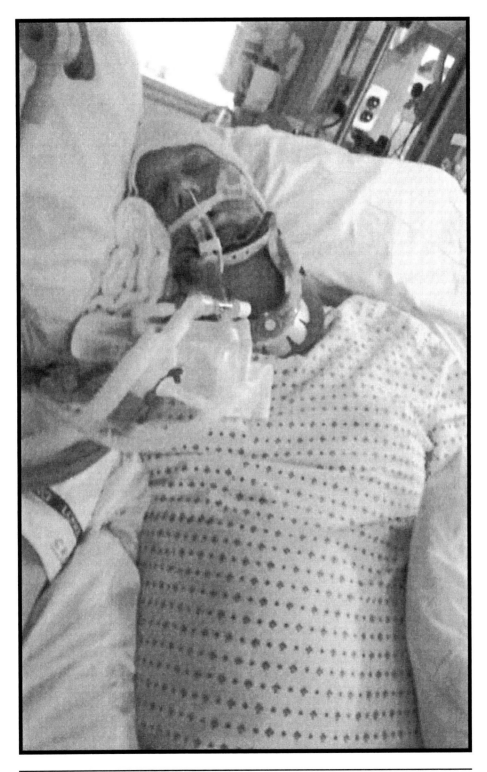

- 2 -

WITH PASSION AND PURPOSE

"If you deliberately plan to be less than you're capable of being, then I warn you that you'll be unhappy for the rest of your life."

Abraham Maslow

LIFE HAPPENED. You might be wondering; what was the life Matt Potratz lived when life happened? Who am I and how did I get here?

I grew up in the small town of Pierce, Idaho which is in the heart of the beautiful Clearwater Mountains. When I say small, I mean it. Like, to the tune of population 744 and even less today. I married my high school sweetheart at the age of only 18. She loved God, loved the outdoors and loved me so I figured we were set for life. Because of the unique location of our hometown, we had both grown to love the outdoors. We spent a lot of time in the back-country together hunting, fishing, camping, hiking, and—saving the best for last—riding snowmobiles.

Discovering My Passion

My passion for the outdoors started at a young age. As young boys, my two brothers and I spent plenty of time in what we called the "woods" building forts, bike trails, and eventually riding dirt bikes. In high school, we'd go camping, hunting, fishing; anywhere our old beat up Toyota pickups would take us. My parents owned and operated a small resort—which encouraged our love for the outdoors even more as sportsmen came and went in all seasons.

Because of its mountainous location, Pierce was home to significant snowpack in the wintertime. This brought in many groups of snowmobilers to enjoy the Idaho powder snow. The area was also home to a vast trail system over a variety of terrain, creating a demand and need for my dad to launch a snowmobile rental fleet. On slower days, my dad would take us boys out and let us give the machines a try. Whenever the opportunity arose, I would tag along with a group riding from the resort, acting as their unofficial guide to our incredible mountain areas.

It was during my senior year of high school that I began to really enjoy the sport. I made a plan that when I graduated, I would work while attending college and invest in my own machine. So, I did just that. Being young and dumb as I was, I decided I needed a brand-new snowmobile. I visited my credit union for a loan, marched down to the local Ski-Doo® shop in my college town and purchased my first new snowmobile.

Every time I had a day off from school and work that winter, I was back in Pierce and on the snow. I would regularly take groups from the resort on more tours of the area. I knew our mountains very well so I would lead the group to either the best scenery or the best play areas, depending on their request.

Matt and Tim at the "top of the world"

I also met a new friend in college who shared the same ability and passion for the sport. Tim was one of the first guys I found that could truly push me to the next level. I was usually the one doing the pushing, so I found excitement in finding someone with the same drive that I had—plus even better riding ability—to push me to become better.

We spent a lot of time on the snow together. He showed me around his home riding area, and I showed him around my home turf. I still believe today that he is one of the most talented, undiscovered riders in the sport. In fact, one of the things I love about him is that *undiscovered* is exactly the way that he wants it to be. He doesn't want to be in the spotlight. We saw a ton of amazing country together and went a lot of dangerous places that I'm sure we shouldn't have. The more seat time I gained, the more I grew to love the sport. I put 3,800 miles on my new sled that first season, and that's where it all began.

After business school at Lewis-Clark State College, my wife Sarah and I returned home to Pierce to join my parents in the local business climate. The area had recently lost its largest employer, a plywood mill, to the declining timber industry. I had worked at the mill during the summers under their college hire program, so it was difficult to watch them tear it down. In an attempt to help boost the local economy and shift it towards tourism, I

Four Generations of Potratz Boys

launched High Country Sports, a Polaris® and Arctic Cat® dealership. We sold and serviced new and used ATVs and snowmobiles, and operated a rental fleet of both as well. I teamed up with my parents, assumed their rental fleet and provided rentals, parts, and service for their customers.

I also began to feed off of knowledge in the industry, read books, and watch videos to expand my knowledge on specific snowmobile tuning for different altitude ranges and performance enhancement. My business kicked off well and looked promising, but as time went along we couldn't jump start the economy like we'd hoped. After about two years, I made the tough decision to liquidate and get out while I could still avoid potential bankruptcy. Shortly afterward, I got a call from Mountain Motor Sports, the Yamaha® dealer in Orofino (just 35 miles away), asking me to join their team. They had a broader product line with motorcycles, ATVs, snowmobiles, and cargo trailers. I saw it as a great opportunity, so I took the position as their lead salesperson.

We moved to Orofino, bought a house, and decided it was time to start our family. Sarah landed a job using her college education as a math teacher at the local high school, and our first son Connor was born on February 12, 2005. It's hard to describe the feeling as a father when you see that baby boy for the first time and know that he is yours. I'm sure that many of you can relate. I was so proud to be a father.

Since I was now also selling dirt bikes, I started racing in many of the local cross-country races. I changed my race number on my number plates and jersey to 212 in honor of Connor's birthday. He still looks at the pictures today and knows that 212 is his birthday.

I enjoyed riding motorcycles, but snowmobiling was still my passion. Continuing to sell snowmobiles gave me more opportunity to get seat time on the snow. Tim had also relocated after college and was working as service manager for a dealership a couple hundred miles away. We were still riding together whenever we could. He also started riding with a couple groups to see the area close to his new home—and was making quite an impression.

A new film company had just started filming backcountry snowmobiling to produce technical riding highlight films. They were looking to make what are commonly referred to as "extreme riding" films to entertain snowmobilers. Some of the "509 Films" crew would bring their machines to Tim for service.

It wasn't long before the group was making comments like, "You guys are crazy!" or "Are you sure those are just 700's?"

They heard that Tim could ride quite well, and approached him about riding in their first film. He agreed and told them that he also had a friend that they would most likely want on camera. He called me with the story and I agreed that we should give it a shot.

The first ride was scheduled on our home turf, our favorite riding area near McCall. Most of the riders in the film were riding what we call "mod sleds;" heavily modified to enhance performance and weight. The Arctic Cat® M Series® sleds that we were riding, on the other hand, were 700cc and essentially what we call "bone stock." The only modifications to our machines were lightweight exhaust canisters, which are primarily for weight savings and add very little performance. We had also done minor clutch tuning to enhance power delivery to the track. The riders we were meeting up with were riding 900cc to 1200cc machines with a whole laundry list of modifications.

It was late season, so the snowpack was firmed up with a soft melting layer on top. It was the type of snow that we laughed and referred to as "hero snow." You could go nearly anywhere you pointed your machine. Well, as long as you

Matt Potratz

Revelstoke, British Columbia

509 Films

had the ability to pick the right lines and maneuver your machine through the tight stuff—and the guts to take it there.

When we unloaded at the trailhead, the group rumbled up with their high horsepower machines with a list of modifications. "Is that what you're riding today?" they asked dubiously. "What's under the hood?"

"Just stock 700's," we proudly replied. To add some humor, I think I said something along the lines of, "Don't worry, I ate my Wheaties!" Off we went, headed for the mountain—and our first time on camera.

We weren't sure what the day would be like and we thought we just might get our tails kicked by their big bore machines. However, we did have an advantage since it was our stomping grounds and we knew the mountains quite well. It wasn't long before the group was making comments like "You guys are crazy!" or "Are you sure those are just 700's?" We probably pulled a few lines we wouldn't have on an average day, but we did a good job acting as if we knew what we were doing!

One thing viewers like to see are first ascents up "chutes." Chutes, as I described earlier, are just like they sound: outcroppings in the rocks where the snow can lay in the form of a chute, often just a little wider than a snowmobile. I made my first ascent up a technical chute that I had eyeballed but had never pulled the trigger on. That climb, and a handful of good shots that day, gave me a pretty good segment in my first film and their first film. Tim also earned a respectable segment. The name of the movie was a perfect fit: First Ascent. We ended up making some new friends that day, and they were a great group to ride with. It was the start of a great friendship between 509 Films producer and owner, Tom Delanoy, and myself.

When I left the snow that day, I wasn't sure how my riding footage would stack up. Unsure if I would hear from the film company again, I was just happy that I could say I had at least made it into a film. It was something more to talk about when selling and tuning snowmobiles. Sales were really growing in every product line and it was becoming more time consuming to keep up. We were short staffed for the volume so I would often come in early in the morning, break machines out of the crate, do the necessary assembly and setup inspection, change clothes, and be ready to hit the floor when the front doors opened. I would also make the necessary early morning drives to trade product with other dealers in order to get a color or specific equipment requested to make a sale. I didn't mind because I like mornings, but it did become a bit of a drain. Some days would end up being twelve to fourteen hours. I really enjoyed the job, so I considered it worth it. Looking back, at times I made the mistake of allowing the job to consume me. It cost me valuable time and energy I needed to be a good husband and father, but things remained pretty healthy on the home front.

That next winter I *did* get the call to ride with 509 Films again. I made a couple of trips with the film crew and it went quite well. One trip that will forever be a memory—and ended up being the most epic footage of my career—was my first trip to Revelstoke, B.C., Canada. The total snow depth on the upper basin was estimated at about seventeen feet with nearly two feet of fresh powder! Then God decided to give us a big ole' hug by delivering two days of blue sky and sunshine!

I felt right in my element, and my snowmobile didn't miss a beat. Free-rider Rob Alford put us up in his log chalet bed & breakfast and treated us to some country typically only covered by the locals. At the premiere event for the film Vertical Ascent, fellow riders joked that "maybe they should have just called this film 'Matt Potratz,' as I was again blessed with a few great segments.

Time for Change

In February that winter, I made the decision to make a shift in employment. Business was growing rapidly in my third year at Mountain Motor Sports, and I didn't see eye to eye with management on a few core principles. We didn't share the same intensity to keep customer service at the level needed to continue our growth. Sales volume had grown significantly, and I didn't feel that we had the fixed operations support needed for the increased volume. When I humbly approached ownership with my concerns, it quickly became clear we were not on the same page. I was told that I was pushing too hard and growing the business faster than they wanted to grow. I respected that and gave them a one-month notice to find a replacement salesperson.

In truth, I had already considered moving out of the power sports business because the income peak was relatively low and benefits were hard to come by. Employment was limited in Orofino, so I researched some potential businesses to visit with my resume in the city of Lewiston, Idaho—just forty miles down the river. I had printed seven resumes and my first stop was Rogers, the local Toyota®-Scion® dealership. I returned home with six resumes on the seat of my truck; Ryan Rogers had asked me to join his team.

Ryan and I had talked a few times about a snowmobile purchase and met on the snow once or twice. He was surprised to see me on the job market, so the interview consisted of only a few questions about why I had made the decision to leave the power sports industry. "Matt," he concluded, "I've really only got just got one question for you; when can you start?" I explained to him that I had given my current employment a one-month notice. With a smile, he replied, "One month is too long. Change that to two weeks." I agreed, and informed Mountain Motor Sports ownership that next morning.

I honestly never thought I would become a car salesperson. You definitely have a stereotype to fight in that business. But I saw it as a bit of a challenge, a chance to be different than the stereotype and show people a different kind of buying experience.

After I got through the training process, I did just that. I hit the ground running not as a car salesman, but simply as Matt Potratz. Since I had done nothing but sell since age 19, I learned that the *relationship* is the transaction. Everyone has to have a car. Our world is too busy and spread out to walk or ride bicycles everywhere. So, I figured it was just a question of who they were going to buy it from. Utilizing the relationships I had built in the power sports world, the new friends I was making on the car lot and of course some beginner's luck, I delivered seventeen cars in my first full month at Rogers.

I was impressed and comfortable with how process-oriented the dealership was. Following defined processes assured that every customer that came across the curb or in the front door experienced the same level of quality service. It was exactly what I had strived for in power sports, and one of the disagreements I had come up against with ownership in the past. *Good* is not good enough in my book. I wanted every customer that came on the premises, whether their first or fiftieth time, to have the *best* experience that could be delivered. Rich and Ryan Rogers shared that same passion, so I felt right at home.

The first few months, I was commuting the forty miles from Orofino each morning and evening. Our home sold very quickly, so we rented a home until the school year finished up and we could find a desirable home that met our family needs in Lewiston.

I got home from work one day to find Sarah crying on the couch.

"What's wrong?" I asked gently, snuggling up against her.

"I'm pregnant."

"Okay, tough timing I know, but why are you crying?" I replied. "We both want more children."

She shared with me how difficult it was to leave Connor and go to work every day and she hated the thought of leaving two, being a full-time mom and a full-time teacher.

My income was looking promising enough at that point that I confidently told her, "After this school year, I want you to stay home. I believe God will provide. If I have to work a little more to make it happen, I will. I'll find a way to continue to sell enough cars to support our family."

She was a little hesitant, and questioned me some, but I assured her that I would make ends meet. God had given me a passion and drive to be a provider that I still have today. I think most of us men have that deep down desire to be the provider for our families, not just financially, but safety, comfort and security as well. I have always strived to make my home a safe haven and even a shelter from the storms of life. God was the foundation of our home and family, and I wouldn't have it any other way.

Soon, Sarah notified the school district that she was leaving, and we took a leap of faith. We moved to Lewiston, bought a beautiful home in a great, family-oriented neighborhood, landed in a great new church and car sales were paying the bills. Life was good.

After only about eighteen months as a salesperson, I was averaging fourteen cars per month and bringing home a comfortable income. I was enjoying it, but I had a desire to eventually be involved at the leadership level and owner-ship was aware of that. In fact, Ryan had asked me in my interview, "What are your future plans? Where do you see yourself say 5 years from now?"

"Working here but not selling cars," I had replied without hesitation. "I hope to be helping you manage the dealership."

"Okay, perfect," Ryan said with a smile.

Then, a position opened: Finance Manager, handling all of the title work and financing for each car deal. When Ryan offered me the position, I initially hesitated and asked quite a few questions. My income was supporting my family well and I wanted to make sure I wasn't taking more responsibility for less or the same compensation. He assured me that I would most likely be ahead financially by making the move.

There were two of us, one for each sales team and schedule. The training process was smooth, and I quickly picked up on the procedures and responsibilities. My partner, J.W., had been a big influence in my walking in with a resume a year and a half prior. He was a customer of mine in power sports. When he found out I was unhappy, my phone rang with something like, "Get your butt down here and talk to Ryan!" J.W. ended up becoming one of my best friends—and still is as I write this book.

> *I did a pretty good job of investing quality time in my boys, but I failed when it came to investing in my wife.*

The new position went very well and I was learning something new every day. As a team, we made the department productive and profitable. After only a few short months, another position came open: New Vehicle Sales Manager. Ryan knew that I was a good fit for the position because of my passion for leadership. Best of all, this would get me back out on the front line with the salespeople. Soon, I began to take on more training, more responsibilities—and another new job description.

In this chair I would manage all of the ordering: model, color, and equipment mix of our new Toyota inventory, as well as serving up the deal structure including trade amounts, payments, etc. I would also lead a team of sales people on a daily basis. I deliberately say lead, not manage. One of the great quotes by Benedict Arnold that I lived by from day one as a manager was, "You manage process; you lead and develop people." People are not a process, not a 'thing.' We are each a *person* with a unique personality and unique motivations. We all need leadership at some point.

I took the time to develop relationships with each of my team members on a professional and personal level. The message I was striving to communicate was simple yet powerful: "As your leader, I value you." I quickly discovered that the productivity of my people was in direct relation to value. Do I feel valued by my peers, my leader, the dealership? If the answer was yes, they brought their 'A' game. You can read more about that in my next book.

I began to gauge my success not by my own success, but by the success of my people, on the job and at home.

Success at Work, Failure at Home

Although I encouraged my people to find success at home, my own success on the homefront was beginning to suffer. My wife and I had already discovered that our motivation and drive in life was completely different. We came from two completely different family backgrounds. Unfortunately, we did a poor job of communicating through those differences.

Our second son Ethan had been born healthy and perfect on October 21, 2006. I thought life was going great. I had two amazing children, a beautiful home, reliable transportation, and income sufficient enough to allow Sarah to be a stay-at-home mom. Sarah, on the other hand, viewed the picture through a completely different lens. My job was somewhat tasking, both mentally and physically. The hours alone meant sixty plus hours a week away from my family. To make matters worse, I often made the mistake of not laying the job down when I went home. I was still e-mailing, texting, and calling off and on when I should have been one hundred percent focused on my family.

Since riding consumed a large amount of my time in the winter, I chose to sell my motorcycle and gear, stop racing, and free up all of my time off in the summer for my family. I did a pretty good job of investing quality time in my boys, but I failed when it came to investing in my wife. We had already suffered a disconnect when we began to discover that we didn't share the same passion in life, and now my work-a-holic tendencies began to create some spite. I justified it all by telling myself that I had to do it to support my family. We continued on without the much needed communication regarding the issue. I think we both did our best to avoid confrontation, believing that it was best for our marriage and family. However, the spite began to really hurt. Human nature is such that when we get hurt, we want to run. I didn't really run away, but between work and snowmobiling I could always find a way to be gone just a few more hours for whatever reason.

In the busyness of it all, we found out that Sarah was pregnant with our third son. Around the same time, I allowed myself to cross a boundary and break a commitment that I never thought I would. I could try to cover up my mistakes in the words I write, but I believe that you, my reader, deserve to know the complete story. I am still ashamed even as I write these words: I was unfaithful to my wife and got involved with another woman.

I always spoke to the guys at work about the importance of keeping your commitments, at work and in life. Now, I had broken one of the biggest commitments that we make in life. I was crushed. I literally broke my own heart and I still remember weeping as I came clean with my wife. The couch downstairs became my new bed, and we began the process of counseling and prayer to try to clean up the mess.

Although I should have slowed down to focus on the mess I had made, I didn't. That winter I again had tremendous success on the snow. My segments in 509's new movie, Evolution probably stand as my best appearance in a snowmobile film. We were able to capture a great variety of different terrain and riding styles. The sponsorships were starting to come together and my gear and accessories were provided by aftermarket companies at no cost to me.

Late in the season, I started a sponsor relationship with Kirk Zack, owner of HMK Boots & Outerwear. They took care of my boots and riding gear, head to toe. Today that relationship has grown from sponsorship to friendship. I

My Boys: Connor, Ethan & Caleb

also received a call from Phil Yribar, owner of 208 Productions, requesting a segment in his movie, DRY ICE. I agreed and rode with 208 late that spring in McCall aboard my newest addition to the lineup; my turbo-charged Arctic Cat M1000, cranking out over 250 horsepower! And yes, that's a *lot* of power when its driving only a 500 pound machine and myself behind a set of handlebars. At times, just hanging on was a chore!

Earlier that spring, life continued to avalanche on the homefront. I packed up what I needed to live and moved out of my family home—leaving my boys and their mom in a comfortable, safe home, but with no daddy under the roof. It was a very heavy feeling backing out of the garage that day. The separation and eventual divorce came after we had really no progress in counseling or at home. We both admit now that neither one of us wanted to be in it, so we lacked the motivation required to rebuild. We hoped to keep it together for our boys, but it's very difficult when that's your only motivation.

Continuing with my passion to provide, I drew up a plan to cover the cost of living so that Sarah could stay home with our new son Caleb for 12 months. His brothers had been fortunate enough to have a full-time mom there during that baby stage, so I wanted Caleb to have nearly the same experience that his brothers had.

The Giving Tree

After just a couple of years as sales manager, more change, more responsibility, and more leadership opportunities presented themselves. The sales manager that trained me was moved back to a sales position. I would eventually fill the role as the lead manager in the sales department. Ryan and I worked together to prepare me to take the leadership role. He casted vision and expectations, and it was my job to work with our management team to see that they were efficiently executed.

One of our experienced salespeople was selected to train with me to be my partner and lead a sales team. While the personnel changes were taking place, we were also excited to be moving across the lot into our new state of the art dealership facility. Sales had been declining across the industry so it was a stressful time to take on the financial burden of the new dealership. But ownership knew they were committed to it so we operated as productively as we possibly could and made the move with confidence.

As we headed into the winter season shortly after the move, I found time in early February 2009 to film for a day with 509 for an appearance in the movie REVOLUTION. We made plans for another film shoot later that season. But, that film shoot didn't happen. A few weeks later, I stayed at work late on February 28th, 2009 to close out the books for the month. The next morning was my March 1st film shoot in McCall. I was excited for it as the snow conditions were supposed to be excellent. I had no idea what that next day would hold.

> *Who you are can't be taken from you. What you do can all be taken away in an instant.*

Life had been a bit of a roller coaster but was still going quite well. On the job, my employer was still very pleased with me: I had been promoted three times in a two year period. My name was becoming fairly well known on a snowmobile. I was viewed as one of the elite mountain free-riders in the nation. Best of all, my boys were healthy and I still got to be with them often. Matt Potratz was blessed: a proud father to three boys, a musician, a successful sales manager, and a professional snowmobiler.

Let's take a closer look at this. Those things I listed are all great, but they were *what* I was, not *who* I was. Often we make the mistake of wrapping our identity up in all of the things we spend our time doing. The reality is that we can only find our identity in *who we are* inside. So who was Matt, really? A leader, a man of integrity, a caring person, the guy who always invested more in others than in myself, a giver of time, talent, and resources, humble, fun—the list could probably go on.

Mary had given me a book on Valentine's Day, just two weeks before the avalanche. The book THE GIVING TREE was about a tree that gave all that it had to a little boy, right down to its stump—simply because the tree wanted the boy to be happy. When it literally had nothing left to give, the tree was happy. She said that my life was the same story. I was a lot happier and fulfilled when giving, rather than getting, and often gave all that I had.

A Chinese proverb echoes my stance, simply: "To give is more fortunate than to receive." These characteristics are really what define who I am. Because if LIFE HAPPENS on a large enough scale, all of the things I first listed can easily be stripped away. Most of the things in the second list can't be taken from you short of losing your life. *Who you are* can't be taken from you. *What you do* can all be taken away in an instant.

Matt was on top of the world: snowmobiling, work, musician, father, healthy, athletic. It all got stripped away, thrown off a mountainside, slammed into a tree, and buried in an avalanche.

Where do you find your identity? When LIFE HAPPENS to the degree that mine did, I promise you this: you will want to know *who* you are.

– 3 –
HERO TO ZERO

"*Whom God will use mightily, he wounds deeply.*"

Matt Chandler

FROM THE TIME AN AVALANCHE FRACTURED TO THE TIME I WAS VIOLENTLY CRUSHED INTO A TREE AND BURIED, WAS TWELVE SECONDS. Life can definitely change in an instant. Everything had been going quite well for me, but in twelve seconds, I went from *Hero to Zero*.

When my dad initially received that phone call from the top of the mountain, he says that "It was the call I somehow knew, but hoped would never come." The call came; Matt has been caught in a bad avalanche and is unconscious. Later, my dad reflected on his flight from Seattle to Boise:

> *"The most agonizing time in my entire life. There was so much that was unknown. I was told that he was alive—but what if he didn't survive the trip out of the backcountry? So many 'what ifs?' I had to get hold of myself, I needed to be strong, I needed to be there for the rest of the family, I needed to lead them through this crisis.*

> *"Somewhere along that plane ride to Boise, I began to call out to God. Yes, I cried out for Matt's life—but more than that, I cried out for strength and resolve to face whatever might lie ahead. Little did I know, that strength and resolve would be tested to the maximum degree in the coming days."*

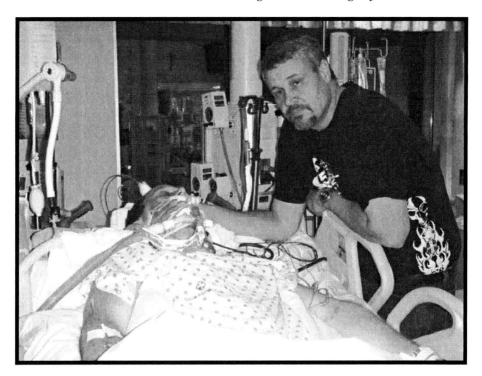

As he looks back on that moment when he walked into my ICU room, he adds:

"My heart became faint as I saw my oldest son lying in a coma, struggling for his very life."

Morning number one of my fight for survival began in the Intensive Care Unit (ICU) with tubes, hoses, and wires on all sides of my body. The doctors couldn't fully understand why I was still unconscious and unresponsive. They began to use painful stimuli, where they would inflict pain on me, looking for some response from my body. Even in the coma state, our bodies should still respond to pain in some way.

> *He picked up my broken leg a few feet off the table—my shattered femur that had not been fully treated yet—and dropped it to fall back against the table.*

They tried several different stimuli with no response, my body laid still on the table. Then, my family was told that they were going to hook a scan to my brain, followed by similar pain infliction. The doctor explained to my parents, "If the scan doesn't show some response from his brain, we're in trouble." They started the scan and began to again inflict pain on my body, but still, the scan showed no response from my brain.

Finally, the doctor tried one last thing that would guarantee a response—if one was there. He picked up my broken leg a few feet off the table—my shattered femur that had not been fully treated yet—and dropped it to fall back against the table. Still, the scan showed no response from my brain.

I don't think the doctor realized Mary was sitting quietly in the chair in the corner of the room. He said to himself, "Well, not much hope here."

She jumped up in shock. "What did you just say?"

"I'm sorry, this just doesn't look good," he replied. He went to the waiting room to tell my family, "I'm sorry. Short of a miracle, Matt's not going to be with us anymore. He's alive; his heart is still beating but only because we're breathing for him and as near as I can tell, he's essentially *brain-dead*."

My dad's heart sunk. "This is it," he thought. "I'm going to be planning my son's funeral." But, as our family leader, he stood strong and collected as he always had, and dug in to find a little piece of firm ground.

He remembers preparing himself for 'crunch time' as the leader of our family. His faith in God was being put to the test. He rounded up the doctor to speak with him more about it and came back with these words:

> *"Doc, I'm not willing to accept that yet. If Matt were in my shoes, he wouldn't give up on me this soon. I would like a second opinion."*

Phone calls, texts, and e-mails again went out across the nation asking people to hit their knees and pray. The word went out even across the world—my mom's parents are world missionaries, and they called their teams overseas to pray.

My dad put together a team to go in my room and pray with me. They had been in the room for an hour or so when my good friend John said to the group, "Guys, I don't know why but I just feel like Matt knows we're in the room. Let's see if *we* can get him to respond." John got right in my face and loudly said, "Matt, it's John. If you can hear me, raise your right leg!"

I couldn't lift my leg but to their surprise, I moved it a little! Wow! They continued by trying to get me to squeeze a hand and eventually I lightly squeezed! They rushed from the room to get the doctor. A few minutes later, he stepped in the room.

"I hear you think he responded?" the doctor said, doubt coloring his tone.

"He did respond!" John said with confidence.

The doctor stepped up to the bed, got right in my face and said loudly, "Matt, if you can hear me, open your eyes!"

I wasn't able to open my eyes, but the doctor's tune changed a little as I undeniably fluttered my eyelids! Eventually, they got me to squeeze his hand a little too! He stepped back from the bed, almost in shock.

"Well Doc, does that mean we just saw a miracle?" John asked.

Never Let Go

I later spoke with my dad about how they felt when the excitement of the miracle faded and they were faced with the reality of the long road still ahead. His e-mail describing his thoughts reads:

> *"The days ahead were not easy as you still had a long road of recovery ahead, but our faith carried us through the 'valley of the shadow of death.' We all seemed to sense that God had a purpose for your life being spared. Therefore, He would give us the strength and the resolve to walk through whatever might lie ahead."*

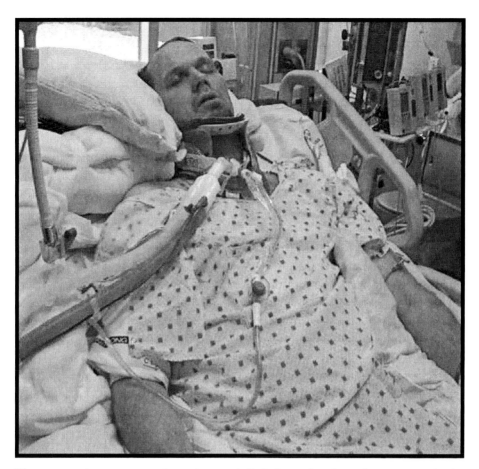

The prognosis was uncertain and essentially left my family with a grim outlook: "Matt is most likely going to survive," they were told, "but we are unsure about the condition of his brain if and when he comes out of the coma." The 'active, on the move Matt' was unresponsive to the world around me. They were unsure of how long I would remain this way. I had friends in and out of the room by my bedside, praying and just being there with me.

My youngest brother Jon (and today my best friend), began his long commitment to be by my side as much as he could be there. His work schedule in the Wyoming Natural Gas field worked him on the rotation of ten days on and then five days off. From day one, he committed to drive the 800 miles roundtrip to be by my bedside on every one of his days off. On his tenth day, he would go to work early, at 1:00 a.m., run his route, then head for Boise to be there for a full five days. I later found out why. He had looked up to me while growing up. He modeled his outlook on life, work ethic, and even beliefs after his big brother. I had been his hero—now it was his turn to be mine.

My sister Jessica, another of my closest friends, discovered something early on that became a great method of connection during the fight to survive. Caring-Bridge.org is a hospital-sponsored website where she could build a "Matt Potratz" page with a quick story of what happened and my medical condition. It allowed family, friends, and fans to follow the battle daily, even hourly. My family could post an update on my condition that became available worldwide at the click of a button. Users could also opt to receive a notification e-mail any time a new update was posted. They could also post comments on the site to encourage my family and friends as they watched me lay unresponsive in the hospital.

Initially, there wasn't a lot to update on the site as I remained in a comatose state. Hours in the coma became days. On day three, I opened my eyes slightly and moved my right leg and arm—but still, no one was home. I was registering some with slight hand squeezes and facial expressions but was unable to focus in on anything. My family refered to it as a "ghosty" type of look. Then I would close my eyes and drift back to unresponsive.

They say I hated it when they would clean my mouth and at times, it motivated me to try to sit up. A very big concern came up that first week: doctors discovered a blood clot that could spell disaster. The clot was in my vertebral artery, which supplies the brain with the blood and oxygen it requires in order to function. "We think that with medication the clot will dissipate," my family was advised, "but it's a serious matter because if the clot suddenly releases, it will most likely mean instant death or a nearly brain-dead condition for life."

My dad says it was hard to go to sleep that night with that hanging in the balance. By the grace of God, the clot dissipated fairly quickly with no complications. In the midst of the immediate concern of the blood clot, I developed pneumonia. Fortunately, it didn't initially plague me as badly as they were concerned that it could, but it did add to the stress on my body. A couple of days in, the antibiotics were working and the CT scan on my lungs looked surprisingly good—yet the pneumonia hung on.

I remained in a coma surrounded by friends and family filling my room with love. My vitals showed that I could sense that love, and they remained at consistent and calm levels. At day seven they started C-pap trials, where they would remove me from the respirator to determine if I could breathe on my own. I did! C-pap results continued to show good signs, as at times I could take multiple deep, steady breaths on my own. Eleven days into the fight, I was able to breathe on my own for three and a half hours. I was showing slow improvement, which was much better than no improvement. When the trauma surgeon visited my room, he commented, "Good things happen slowly, bad things happen fast"—which encouraged my family's patience.

I continued to open my eyes for brief periods, which quickly became an encouraging sign. At no surprise, I did not like being restrained and I was a bit combative at times. At one point, it took five nurses to hold me down and they tell me that I even took a swing at one of them. I was showing signs of being Matt. I don't ever hit women, but no one holds me down for long. *Let's get movin'!*

> *For the first time, I tried to smile! Their voices singing that beautiful song on the phone turned out to be a defining moment in my fight for life.*

To help me breathe better and continue to do so on my own, plans were made for a tracheotomy to get me off the ventilator. My body also needed consistent nutrient intake, so it was time to put in a supply line. On Tuesday, March 10th—nine days in—the trache breathing tube and a feeding tube were successfully installed to make it more comfortable for me if I started to come around more, and to prevent damage to my vocal chords from the ventilator.

Plans were also made to move me from ICU to the Rehab and Recovery unit. However, circumstances changed; the tube installs took their toll on me. I opened my eyes very little and wasn't very responsive. Over just a few days out of the ICU, my heart rate jumped up and my fever cranked up the heat. In addition, the pneumonia took a turn for the worse and I developed a bladder infection and impacted bowels—all of which were taking away much needed energy to fight. The decision was made to wheel me back to the ICU. The trip back to the ICU seemed like a step in the wrong direction, but I responded well to the move and things began to settle to normal levels again.

During that struggle, something happened that will never be forgotten in my lifetime, or theirs. My boys had not seen me yet at this point, as it had been decided that it would be quite scary seeing dad in that condition and hooked to so much equipment. I hadn't really responded to the world yet. Even though my eyes opened a little, my brain wasn't registering my surroundings. They were simply told, "Daddy got hurt really bad and just needs to sleep for a while."

As a musician, I often played my acoustic guitar and would sing songs with my boys. They would join in to sing and dance to the sound of my guitar. Their favorite song to sing was a song by Matt Redman called "You Never Let Go." They would sing out the chorus:

"Oh no, you NEVER LET GO through the calm and through the storm.
Oh no, you NEVER LET GO, in every high and every low.
Oh no, NEVER LET GO. Lord, you NEVER LET GO of me."

Since they just thought that I was sleeping, their mom asked them if they would like to call daddy to see if I could hear them talk to me while I was sleeping.

Connor, my oldest boy, spoke up. "We don't want to call Daddy to talk to him," he said. "Let's call and see if he can hear us sing to him."

"Oh!" Sarah replied. "What song should we sing?"

"Our favorite song: Never Let Go," Connor said immediately.

So they called, the cell phone was placed to my ear, and my boys sang "Never Let Go" to their daddy in a coma. I have no memory of it, but there was no doubt that I heard my boys. I raised my eyebrows and for the first time, I tried to smile!

The best part is that their voices singing that beautiful song on the phone turned out to be a defining moment in my fight for life. It was a turning point. Although remaining mostly unconscious, I began to respond more my surroundings in different ways. It became noticeable based on my movements and demeanor that I was at least aware that someone was near me or talking.

However, as they began to encourage my body to move more, it was becoming more apparent that my left arm was limp as I didn't move it at all. There were suspicions that my arm had sustained significant nerve damage, which could be involved in the lack of movement. Doctors also warned that although it looked as if I might eventually come out of coma, we had a long uphill battle to fight. Because of the spinal injury and neurological damage, they were unsure if I would ever walk again.

I remained in a comatose state; my brain simply wasn't aware yet that I was alive. I still showed signs of awareness of activity around me, but was unable to provide a definite response to stimuli. And then, twenty days in, I finally looked alive! My eyes were not ghostly, not glassy—no, this was different! I have no memory of it but my family recalls the events of the breakthrough. At first they thought they were imagining things, but no, Matt was actually awake

My youngest brother Jon and I

and somewhat aware for the first time in nearly a month! I was back! I was able to recognize friends and family in the room. I tried to talk but communication was limited to hand signals.

Then, something more heart wrenching happened. As they showed me pictures of my boys, I responded with big, meaningful smiles! It was clear to them that my memory was still somewhat intact. However, their hearts sank in agony as the excitement soon faded; I closed my eyes and slipped back into my unresponsive state.

I began to come out briefly, then drift back in. On March 24, I apparently decided it was time to get up. My mom was sleeping peacefully on the couch, but as I'm sure I had done plenty while growing up, I rudely awakened her. She didn't have to knock any sense into me, I took care of that. I got my leg up over the bed rail and managed to pull myself out for a crash on the floor. Thankfully, there were no additional injuries.

They soon learned that we were only half way through the battle. The brain injury had taken its toll and that became very clear on day twenty seven when the doctors replaced my trache tube with a smaller one which allowed me to speak. The words I spoke in my soft, broken voice were only the vocabulary of a child. Regardless, excitement still filled the air because I had spoken for the first time! They got me out of my hospital scrubs and dressed me in a t-shirt and basketball shorts, yet another way to encourage me to get up and go!

The next day, I not only sat up, but pushed it a little further for a very brief stand. I was also able to speak to my boys for the first time. Their mom commented that as Connor heard my voice on the phone, he was very wide eyed and said "Daddy talked!" It would still be a long road to get Daddy back but after nearly a month, I was finally on that road!

To finish the month well, they were able to remove the trache tube and I breathed room air efficiently enough to get sufficient oxygen into my blood! On the last day of the month, I was able to eat solid food for the first time in thirty days. It was ground chicken and fruit. I proved to be processing thoughts well enough to tell Jon, "This chicken is not good." Little did I know, I had plenty of ground hospital food left to eat.

My cousin Joey flew up from California and he and Jon decided we should celebrate the breakthrough with a short wheel chair ride. They wheeled me to a large window where I could look outside. I saw the world that had still been turning, even when my world had slowed to a minimal rotation.

My brain was still in a partially comatose state and at times I had a hard time processing thoughts and recognizing people. But overall, doctors were very pleased with my progress. Then, my family got to see some of the Matt that they had known before.

On April 2, I was able to call my dad on the phone for the first time. He commented to friends:

> *"It really gave me peace that everything will be okay. It's one thing to hear a positive report from those with him but it was amazing to hear his voice and know in my heart that he is going to come out of this. To hear him say, "Thanks for all the prayers," and "I love you Dad," brought joy to my heart and tears to my eyes."*

To kick off month number two, I started to act and appear even more like me! I want to share with you a few of the posts that my sister wrote in the Caring-Bridge journal on one of her visits.

On April 3rd, she wrote:

> *Good morning, this is Matt's sister Jessica writing the update today as I'm here with Matt and thought it would be nice to have first-hand updates.*
>
> *First of all, I have to say "wow!" It's been nearly four weeks since I last saw him and what an improvement! It was wonderful to see him alert, talking,*

smiling, laughing and even telling jokes! Speaking of jokes, he played a good one on my mom on April Fool's day; one of the therapists told him it was April Fool's Day on Wednesday and suggested that he pull a prank. So, when mom came in that morning, he said "Hi, how are you?" and then said "Who are you?" She was stunned and said, "Matt, you don't know who I am?" He proceeded to lead her on for a couple minutes and then said "April Fools." The joke has been the talk of the rehab floor, but best of all, it indicates that he is able to plan something and carry it through which according to his medical staff, is excellent progress!

As far as his rehab, Matt is doing really well. Yesterday, he stood several times with the physical therapist, went for a long wheel chair ride and then sat up for another 15-20 minutes or so. While he was sitting, we were supposed to keep him pre-occupied so we asked him to sing for us. He sang "Amazing Grace" and then started singing "My chains are gone... I've been set free..." (the Chris Tomlin version). Then he sang "Never Let Go," his boys' favorite song. That started him into talking about his boys. "It's great being a dad," he told the therapist.

Later in the evening, we heard a typical Matt thing when the nurse jumped on him for trying to take a bandage off, he said "Woh, woh, woh—don't hyperventilate!" Does that sound like the old Matt or what?

I'll close for now. Thank you all for your prayers and wonderful support. You all are much of the reason, he is making such excellent progress!

The following day she updated friends on more of the activity and progress that she witnessed. On day thirty five behind hospital walls, she shared:

Good afternoon! It's Jessica here again bringing you another update. Jon had to leave yesterday morning and Matt cried when he left; that made us all cry. Jon has been a huge help to Matt and inspires him to push harder and get better. He's not only a good brother, but an awesome friend!

Matt had another good day yesterday in physical therapy, sitting up in his wheel chair for about an hour and a half. Sitting up is very exhausting and towards the end, he began to experience a lot of pain. He took a good nap in the afternoon and was back to his fun-loving self in the evening. I think the staff enjoys working with him because of his humor and because he's so polite; he always wants to know everyone's name and says "thank you" to anyone who helps him.

Connor,

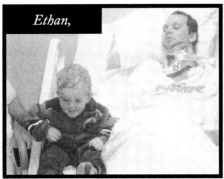

Ethan,

and Caleb

Jessica and I

This morning, he sat in the wheel chair for over an hour again as Mary and I took him around the rehab facility. He loves getting out of the room.

He told us he thought he could probably go home pretty soon since he's been working so hard in physical therapy. He has been working hard; I had the opportunity to sit in on the physical therapy session and got to see him stand up a couple times.

Also, he's finally eating enough to stop being fed through a tube and is on a regular diet so he gets to choose his own food off of a menu... that's a welcome change for him.

Before she went home, she gave a last update. She was excited to be witnessing a miracle; my brain wasn't supposed to fully heal, but slowly, it appeared to be! On Palm Sunday, she wrote:

It's beautiful day here on Palm Sunday in Boise! Matt is doing well and has enjoyed the company he's had this weekend. Thanks to everyone who's been here! Thanks to Tim and Chrissy and the good people at Rogers Toyota, Matt now has framed pictures for his room!

Over the past few days, I have been involved in some priceless conversations with Matt. We have begun to share with him more details about his accident and about all of you people who are supporting him daily with caring words and prayers. He is over-whelmed by how blessed he is and he gives God all the glory. Last night, he said, "There's a great God in heaven watching down on me." Today he shared with us that he never realized how many people he knows and he's realized here in the hospital that he needs to use that influence to tell people how great God is. He says "God saved me for a reason." The following is a direct quote that Matt asked me to write:

"I know now more than ever there is a God watching over me every day. God was absolutely watching over me the day of the avalanche. God is the reason I'm alive!"

One last experience that Jessica got to share with me is one that will never be forgotten. On April 6th, tears were shed as I finally got to see my three Potratz boys for the first time since the end of February.

The boys were somewhat reserved and in awe seeing daddy with braces on and laying in a hospital bed. They soon smiled when they discovered that daddy's bed is motorized and it moves! The pictures you see on the preceding page show three happy boys who get their daddy back.

Hospital Easter Service

My dad came down with friends to join my brother Chris and spend Easter Sunday with me. We had a service in my room to celebrate Christ's resurrection. It was a very moving time as we had a reading from the gospel of Luke, a testimony from Chris, written testimony from Jon, Jessica, and her husband Chris all sharing how Jesus has changed their life and what He's shown them through my tragedy.

I brought the room to tears when my weak voice began to sing the chorus of another powerful song by Matt Redman:

"Once again I look upon the cross where you died.
I'm humbled by your mercy and I'm broken inside.
Once again I thank you, once again I poor out my life."

from ONCE AGAIN, *by Matt Redman*

We ended by sharing communion together.

Although at one point I had told Jon that I was never getting back on a snow-mobile ever again, I informed the crew that Sunday that I was going to get right back in the saddle and climb those big chutes with no intimidation.

My New Battle

Looking back and discussing that month long fight through a coma with friends who were there, I've realized how often in life that we overlook what really matters. When in my coma, very little talk (if any) was about Matt the athlete, the musician, or sales manager. Rather, it was about *who* I was as a father, friend, individual, and the lives I had touched.

Are we placing value on the things in life that really matter, or on things that can be ripped from our grip in twelve seconds? There's a reason we're called human *beings*, not human *doings*.

I wasn't the talented, athletic snowmobiler I had been, but I was still Matt. I had fought death, but now the real work would begin. Because of the trauma from the accident, the poor oxygen supply to the brain during rescue attempts, and the time spent in the coma, my brain suffered significant damage. I would need time for my mind to heal, and for a while I was still like a child in a man's body. My speech was often slurred and I had a shallow vocabulary. My first writing was merely scribbly lines. They would show me flash cards to begin to redevelop my thought processing and comprehension skills. Ten years prior I had graduated high school as student body president, an honor student and class salutatorian. Now, here I was—back at elementary level. Even though I was showing signs of being me again, it was inconsistent and often appeared that I would never be the same "Matt" again.

Physically, I had an uphill battle as well. I was confined to a wheelchair as I was unable to walk due to the left leg neurological damage and subsequent balance problems. I was still in a neck brace due to instability in my spine. My left arm was also still motionless. The docs were pretty certain it was nerve damage, but unsure of the severity; time would tell. What would develop into one of my most difficult battles began to surface as medication intake tapered down. Although motionless and numb, my left hand flared in intense, 24 hour, burning pain. Medication kept it bearable but my doctors couldn't explain why it was happening. They knew it was nerve pain, but were unsure of the source.

In the middle of April, the decision was made to stabilize my spine. A surgeon fused C4-C6 to prevent the vertebrae from shifting forward and putting pressure on the spinal cord which would lead to further complications. A titanium plate was secured to the front of my spine to ensure that if my activity level increases, there will be no unwanted movement.

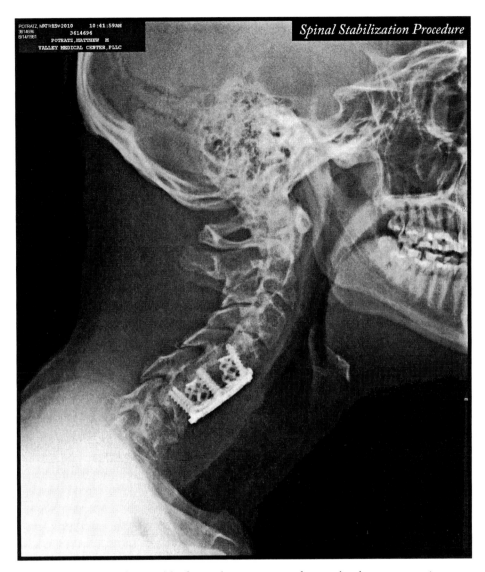

I recovered relatively quickly from the surgery and went back to my routines with the hope of eventual removal of my neck brace. Each day I would undergo physical, cognitive, occupational and speech therapy for as many hours as I could handle and it was absolutely exhausting. However, even at my elementary level I knew that it had to be done.

People have always referred to me as a "fighter." Now it was my only option. I had to fight, or I would never be me again. There were days that I would cry in frustration and although I knew it was just the beginning of a long battle, I just wanted it to be over.

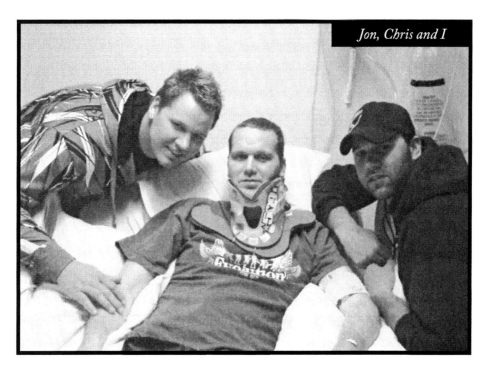

Jon, Chris and I

My Most Valuable Asset: Friends and Family

"In prosperity, our friends know us. In adversity, we know our friends."

(Unknown)

My family and friends responded! My Mom, Carol quit her job and moved to Boise to be by my side and fight the fight with her son. My Dad, Mike came from Seattle as often as he could break away from work. My sister, Jessica came to visit from Lynden, Washington as much as she could. My middle brother Chris came from Reno, Nevada and of course, Jon was with me from Wyoming for a week every ten days.

Mary made the five hour road trip with any spare time she could. There would be some long days and weeks for her as she was a full time mom, business owner, and college student.

Mary was a true friend and was dedicated to being my biggest fan and joined the fight. I had made an impact in her life and now she was prepared to impact mine when I needed it the most.

Then there was my good friend and co-worker J.W. who had to stay back and help keep the work-front running smooth. However, he took every chance he got to come be by my bed and cheer me on.

Ryan Rogers sat by my bed for some good conversations. I asked him a bunch of questions about work and he finally said, "Matt, don't worry about work. I want you to focus on the job at hand here. Let's get you back going again." "But Matt," he went on to say, "I will say this: sometimes we tend to overlook what people do and question their productivity. I know that sometimes I even questioned how you were spending your time at work. When without warning Monday morning hit and Matt was gone, your department nearly imploded upon itself. So, I guess I'm telling you that I'm sorry that it took this to show me how much you do for us there."

Hundreds of people followed my recovery and prayed for me daily. I was surrounded by people who believed in me and also believed in the power of God to bring me through.

How's Your PMA?

Every day I would go through the routine: relearning balance, coordination, comprehension, math, reading, writing, and speech. As my brain began to heal and mature, I had to truly learn the power of a good attitude and a smile. It is said that a positive mental attitude will create more miracles than any wonder drug, and it's true!

At a basketball camp I attended in high school, every morning they would holler out across the gym, "How's your PMA?!?" We had learned that PMA was Positive Mental Attitude and we didn't dare to try to play ball without it. I didn't dare to play this new game without it, either. So I would ask myself that question in the hospital almost daily: "Matt, how's your PMA?"

There was also another simple phrase that I hung onto during the battle and still do today. It was on the inside cover of my binder at work: "Focus on the things you can change." I would often remind myself, "Matt, you can't change the avalanche. You can't change how bad it hurt you. You can't change that you're stuck behind the walls of a hospital." What I could change was my response to the situation. I could change now, today; but not yesterday.

This was when I began to learn the difference between reacting and responding. I pushed myself to respond, not react and to go in one direction only: forward. I believe in God's promise in the Bible when He says in Jeremiah 29:11:

> "For I know the plans I have for you. They are plans for good and not for disaster, to give you a future and a hope."(NLT)

I held onto that hope for a brighter future and kept climbing. At times, I even climbed a little too high. I remember getting a special sign on my door because

I wouldn't stay in bed when I was supposed to. I was trying to get up and go some more. The nurses said, "Matt, sometimes we have a hard time getting people motivated to get out of bed for therapy. You, on the other hand, are a different story. We can't get you to stay in bed to get the rest you need."

I learned the hard way on March 1st, 2009 that life can change quickly. There is a great quote that says, *"You can do something in an instant that will give you heartache for life"* (Unknown). Although I may deal with physical and emotional pain on a daily basis, I make the choice to allow my pain and heartache to make me better. I was put in a situation that I didn't want to be in.

David Foster describes a critical choice we have in a tough situation:

> *"Situations are created when we find ourselves between the way things are and the way they ought to be. While situations differ greatly in size and severity, the core choices they prompt always remain the same; will this make me bitter, or better?"*

I had three amazing Potratz boys counting on Daddy to choose 'better.'

– 4 –
DISCIPLINE OR REGRET

"The way to defeat fear is to decide on a course of conduct and follow it. Keep so busy and work so hard that you forget about being afraid."

Dale Carnegie

MONTH NUMBER THREE CONFINED TO THE HOSPITAL WOULD BEGIN WITH THE SAME DAILY ROUTINE OF MEDICATION, THERAPY, AND REST. Rest alone had become a big part of my recovery. The shell shock from the tremendous trauma my body had undergone left me needing plenty of rest. My brain was healing, but it was becoming more evident to me than to family and friends that it had a lot of healing left to do. I just didn't feel like myself.

At times, I knew my mind was operating at an elementary level but I felt I could do nothing to change it. However, I tuned it out whenever they told me that my brain may never completely heal. I refused to believe it and looked for ways to exercise my mind and find the *Matt* that I knew existed. It was not easy and at times, the frustration took me to tears. But as David Foster says, *"No one coasts up a mountain any more than they can drift upstream."* I would pray the same prayer every morning: "God, give me the strength and courage to make it through another day."

A New Mountain

When riding, I used to laugh and say "Mountains were made to be climbed." I had climbed some of the biggest mountains in the Northern Rockies behind the handlebars of a snowmobile, but now I had an entirely different mountain to climb. I was learning each day to climb the mountain of recovery behind the handlebars of faith. My brain injury was proving to be the most difficult climb of my lifetime.

> *I made the choice to remove "I can't" and "I won't" from my vocabulary and I still avoid those phrases today.*

I remember my dad telling me in sports growing up to "keep my head in the game." Keeping my "head in the game" was a big part of my mental and physical rehabilitation battle. It was quite challenging to keep a malfunctioning head "in the game." In fact, I couldn't do it all my own. My family became my coaching staff and reminded me daily to keep my mind in the right place.

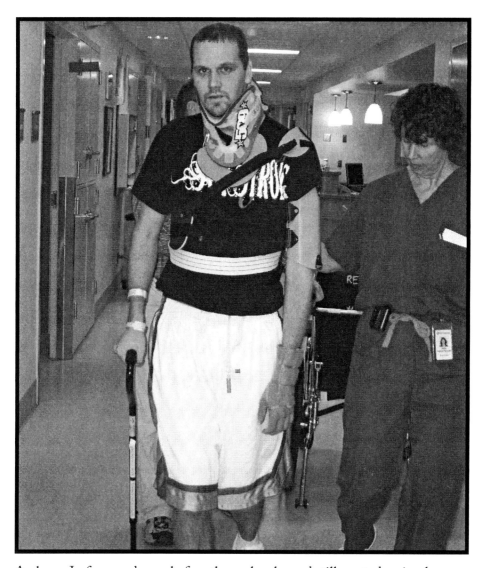

A phrase I often used even before the avalanche and still use today simply states, *"You are what you think,"* and it's so true. I was only as strong as I thought I was. I could only put a smile on every day and go again, if I thought I had a reason to. I was only going to recover as far as I thought I could.

The only way to truly keep my mind in the right place was to also keep my attitude in the right place. I made the choice to remove "I can't" and "I won't" from my vocabulary, and I still avoid those two phrases today. There were definitely times when those phrases came to mind, but with the encouragement of the amazing people God surrounded me with, I was able to take a breath, re-focus, and keep climbing.

React or Respond?

I was forced to make a crucial choice, a choice we all have to make when we face adversity: will I react, or will I respond? Whether we're faced with ordinary, or extraordinary circumstances, consciously or subconsciously, we make this choice. There is a subtle difference in definition, but a massive difference in action. Reacting is generally surrendering control of the situation; washing our hands clean of responsibility. A reaction for me would have been to simply rest through it and make everyone aware that I don't have the strength to push through the recovery routine. A reaction to my non-stop intense nerve pain would have been to beg for more pain medication and allow it to debilitate me.

Responding is proactive and preceded by thought. It is analytical in that you analyze your difficulty, then make a decision as to the best actions needed to recover the lost ground. My response was to wake up each day, harness the energy that I had, and apply it where it was most affective in my recovery. I went as long and hard as I could, then rested. I awoke, and repeated, hour by hour, day by day. God gave me the strength, and I made the choice to apply that strength.

I think you'll agree that nearly every move we make in life is preceded by choice. The choice between these two actions will significantly affect your days, even your life. When you react to life's circumstances, big or small, you allow the circumstance to affect you. When you respond, you affect the circumstance.

Breaking all the Rules

It helped to reach the point that I could go for wheel chair rides and walks outside. It's amazing how something as simple as fresh spring air, or the sound of leaves in the wind can be almost spiritual. I promise you, nearly all of us at some point lose appreciation for the little things in life.

With Jon piloting the wheelchair and myself in the captains' seat, we managed to put our heads together to break the rules on our rides. We went too fast, did some curb hopping, and we were sure to get the front end off the ground, bringing us some much needed, healthy laughter. Our motorcycles and snow-mobiles had spent plenty of time with their front ends in the air so it only seemed appropriate to put the wheel chair there as well.

I remember him taking me to his truck in the parking lot to show me his latest modification. He had been pulling a road drag at work and had a little mishap that was worth a story. The drag had gotten hung up, tightening the chain, then a quick release flung the big heavy steel drag back to his truck and caved in the tailgate. The damage brought us another laugh and I was sure to let him know that I was proud of him.

Hope on the Horizon

The third month of rehab continued and each day showed signs that home was getting closer. I remember how exciting it was to finally tackle the small flight of stairs up and down with no assistance. My physical therapist also added a new piece of equipment to the mix a few times a week. The sports games on the balance board offered by the Nintendo® Wii™ turned out to be a great way to help me with coordination and balance. I would ski, bowl, and play a pretty difficult balance game. Even though I struggled with it, it was fun compared to the daily battle I was fighting!

We began to talk about the possibility of transferring me closer to home to continue my rehab. Plans were eventually made to transfer to St. Luke's Rehabilitation Institute in Spokane, Washington. It was estimated that I would need an additional three to four weeks of in-patient therapy and could then go home to continue out-patient therapy. We determined that it would be much easier for friends and family, especially my boys if I was two hours from home instead of six.

I was not yet in the place mentally or physically to make the flight to Spokane on my own. My good friend Steve who lives in the Spokane area stepped up to the plate and made the trip with me. He paid both fares, flew down from Spokane to Boise, and accompanied me on the flight. It was awesome to be at the airport, back out in the world after three months behind the walls of the hospital. I slowly hobbled around with a cane and we shopped a bit, went out to eat, and I was grinning from ear to ear the entire time.

Soon, however, reality began to set in. I knew that after my flight I was headed for a new set of walls, but Iwould still be behind walls. The flight went well, although the nerve pain increased with altitude. We met Mary at the Spokane airport and she drove me downtown to check in at the rehabilitation institute.

A New Miracle

I was concerned when we went behind locked doors that required security clearance, and soon found out why. Because of my traumatic brain injury, I was classified and placed in a unit with other brain injured patients. Although mine was mild at this point, I was still classified that way. It was difficult enough to go behind walls again, but even more so to go behind locked doors.

That night I cried uncontrollably. "Please take me home, Mary," I begged. "Get me out of this place. I'm well enough to be home. Please, please—please don't make me do this anymore."

"Matt," she said, "I'm sorry, but I can't. You need the therapy. It's important for the long term." After a couple hours of sobbing, I finally settled down to sleep.

In the morning, it quickly became apparent that they had very little idea of the level I was at in my recovery. In their initial tests, they were quite surprised at where I was at both physically and mentally. I also quickly discovered that many on my floor had much more serious affects from their brain trauma. We would dine together to encourage social interaction and work on people skills. We also worked in groups in cognitive therapy. I quickly discovered that I didn't belong there. I would get way ahead of the group in comprehension, math, and reading projects. I remember one time being sent back to my room because I was getting too far ahead of the group. With the type of injury that I had, I wasn't expected to, nor supposed to be doing as well as I was. God had done, and was continuing to do, yet another miracle.

Physically, I was still struggling—but this was to be expected. On the whole, I was staying on schedule for recovery. Much of my recovery was going to simply mean time and repetition. The morning of day five, I met with my doctor to inform him that I wanted to go home.

"Doc," I said, "I don't fit here. My brain is healing and I can walk okay with my cane. I can recover at home."

"Not yet Matt," he said. "You need to keep working at it for a while."

"No, I'm ready to go home."

"Okay," he replied, "We can re-evaluate. I'll give you a chance over the next few days to prove it."

"Prove It."

I was scheduled that same day for my first official 'day out,' where I could have the afternoon and evening to get out in public to shop, eat out, and do what I preferred—under supervision of course. The best thing was that I could be accompanied by Mary instead of hospital staff.

"The first thing I'm gonna do is get a real haircut," I told Mary. So, we did just that at the mall and shopped around a bit just for fun. We also ate lunch—only my second chance to skip hospital food in over one hundred twenty meals!

I took the doctor's "Prove it" statement to heart, and did just that. I had been following the same routine of medication, therapy, and rest for a long time. Jeffrey Gitomer said it well when he simply stated, *"Don't spend your time. Invest your time."* I didn't just float through my daily routine in hopes for the time to pass and the day to end. I did the routine properly and gave it all that my weak body and spirit could give. I had been *proving it* since I was coherent enough to know where I was actually at. But, now was my chance to give it more throttle—to prove my way out of these walls and get back home.

The next morning I got up early, showered myself, got dressed, and arrived early to the cafeteria for breakfast. I had a different kind of focus. I was going to prove that I was ready go home, and I saw no other alternative. I focused on my balance and consistency in physical therapy. I made an extra effort to be independent throughout the day. I again got sent back to my room during cognitive therapy for being too far ahead of the group. I struggled some in speech therapy, but that was something I could continue to work on from home.

The next morning, I got up early and prepared for my day. I continued to pray that same prayer I had prayed every morning since coherent enough to understand what I was fighting: "Lord, give me the strength and the courage to get through another day." He always answered that prayer. It was a Friday when the doctor had challenged me to prove it. The following Monday there was already talk about evaluating me for discharge.

> *"Discipline weighs ounces, while regret weighs tons."*

My doctor informed me that he would meet with my therapists the following morning to evaluate my progress and discuss the possibility of a Wednesday discharge. Once again, I started my Tuesday early, arrived to breakfast early, and was awake and ready for my first therapy session. After my morning therapy, they informed me that my doctor wanted to meet with me.

It's hard to describe the feeling of hearing the positive reports the doctor had received from my therapists and to hear him say, "We've made the decision to prepare discharge papers for midmorning tomorrow. We would also like to do the EMG we have been planning to do before you leave." An EMG was a nerve activity test to determine to what degree the nerves were functioning in my left arm. They previously conducted the same test in Boise with little or no activity. I returned to my room with a smile on my face and opened the folder full of papers that were necessary to get me home.

88 Days

I hardly slept that night thinking back on what I'd been through. Three months prior, I had taken a ride off a mountain that instantly changed my life. Now, I was looking at going back to a world I hadn't seen in *88 days*. I was not the active, athletic man that had left that world. I had an arm that didn't function, I struggled to walk even with a cane, I was very weak, and my body was plagued with debilitating nerve pain. I was finally going home, but the fight was far from over.

I coached myself every morning to stay positive, keep working hard, and keep my mind in the game. I was forced to bring tremendous discipline into my life in order to get out of bed and keep pushing forward after the three months in hospitals. My body was in tear-jerking nerve and muscle pain, and more work meant more pain. But, I had no choice; either do it now—or regret it later. In my opinion, the best business philosopher in history, Jim Rohn, described my situation best when he said:

> *"We must all suffer from one of two pains: the pain of discipline or the pain of regret. The difference is discipline weighs ounces while regret weighs tons."*

I reflected back on all the amazing support that had been shown from family, friends, and even those who didn't really know me. My sister told me on the phone that the number of visitors on Caring Bridge had surpassed twenty five thousand. "Are you sure?" I asked. "How can that be?" I was overwhelmed with appreciation that people had cared enough to think about me and check on me over *25,000* times.

I hadn't remembered the pain and discomfort brought on by the EMG. They attached several probes to my arm which I couldn't feel, due to lack of sensation. The discomfort came when the test started. They had to electrically shock my arm from my hand and then record the reading from the probes. The test results were not very encouraging. The doctor said there was trace activity but that the test had given us no real prognosis. He said nerves just take time to heal and we'll just have to *"wait and see."*

"How long do we wait?" I asked.

"Probably eighteen to twenty-four months and see if you regain some function in that time. If not, do some more tests," he replied.

I could sense a lot of uncertainty and he even admitted it was difficult to predict with nerves, and that the injury appeared to be complex. He also gave no prognosis on my intense nerve pain, just more uncertainty; and again the message: *wait and see.* I don't think I thought much about it at the time because I just wanted to get on with my morning and go home! Soon, Mary and I loaded my stuff and down the road we went.

We talked a lot on the way home about what "home" had been like over the last three months just to catch me up. We shared some serious moments, and some laughter. Breaking over the hill to begin the descent into Lewiston was spiritual. From the top of the hill, you can look across the entire valley and see the cities of Lewiston, Idaho and Clarkston, Washington just across the river. I'd taken in the view hundreds of times, but on this day it was breathtaking!

God wasn't done with me yet. I nearly went home to see Him, but instead, through multiple miracles, He brought me back to my *temporary* home, until my work on earth is done.

– 5 –

THE CHANGING ALTITUDE

"Attitude determines altitude."

David Foster

MY DOCTORS RECOMMENDED THAT I HAVE SOME ASSISTANCE AT HOME, SO MARY OFFERED TO LET ME STAY WITH HER UNTIL I GOT BACK ON MY FEET AND BACK TO WORK. We arrived and *finally* settled me into a *house*; not a *hospital*.

Life was so different! I was always "Mr. On-the-Go," but now was forced to spend most of my day time in the recliner with an entirely new perspective on life. I still needed help up and down stairs, in & out of the shower, etc. I struggled to speak properly and many times I slurred my speech. I couldn't write very legibly. My vision was cloudy when attempting to focus on detail such as to read or watch television. I had to listen very closely to process conversation or instruction.

Home was almost overwhelming. My world was a completely different climate. My new climate was not balmy and full of sunshine. I had to wake up and break out the umbrella every morning to walk through the rain, and there would be plenty of puddles in my path. We quickly got a therapy schedule lined up for physical, occupational, and speech therapy, three days a week. I also blocked out time each week to spend with my boys. Their mom was great about helping me do so.

> *"Me and Ethan don't want you to go on a helicopter ride to the hospital ever again because we want to spend time with you."*

Initially, I spent time with them at her house since I couldn't drive. It was difficult to interact with them with a neck brace on, a paralyzed left arm, and walking with a cane but I did my best. Even just *time* with them was awesome. I found myself at times just watching them interact with each other and learn life together. I was seeing things I had looked right past before in the busyness of life.

One day early on, we went for a short walk down the street. My boys made me laugh when they began to refer to my cane as my "walking stick." Connor then spoke up. "Hey daddy, I drew a cool picture of a helicopter that I want to show you when we get home."

"Great, buddy," I replied. "I can't wait to see it. Did you know that daddy went for a helicopter ride?"

His eyes lit up and he said "No, when?" I explained to him that they used a helicopter to get me off the mountain and to the hospital. I could tell by the look on his face that he was processing that thought. Then he said, "Oh. Well, me and Ethan don't want you to go on a helicopter ride to the hospital ever again because we want to spend time with you." My heart was warmed and I nearly laughed and cried at the same time.

Positive Energy

The first step in physical therapy was to work on balance, strength, and function related to the neurological damage in my left leg. We hoped in time to be able to kick the assistance of my "walking stick" so that I would walk on my own. We also did range of motion exercises to keep my left arm fluid. At times, the intense nerve pain in my hand was nearly unbearable, even with heavy medication. I was dealing with "wait and see" for motor function and really had no answer outside of medication for the nerve pain. I remember saying and thinking often, "I guess I just keep on keepin' on."

I did just that. Each morning I would wake up and go again, focused and passionate about getting my life back. I had survived but life as I knew it was gone, and sometimes seemed out of reach. I remained positive and assured myself that it was just a storm, a season of life, and that it would pass.

Dad, My Boys, and I

I could have been easily distracted to dwelling on what I don't have, haven't done, don't know, and can't do. That mindset would only produce more of the same. Instead, my focus was not on my hand that didn't work, but on the hand that does! I didn't get wrapped up grumbling and complaining that I hobbled around on a cane, I wasn't in a wheelchair! The nerve pain was grueling, but I had my brain back enough to process that pain and take care of myself through it. I disciplined myself to think about everything that I *do have* instead of piling on all the *don't haves.*

Hope became a key ingredient in my recovery. Every day was honestly a fight and I grew to understand that without hope, there was nothing to fight for. I began to envision myself living a normal life and enjoying each moment. I would also envision walking without a cane and being able to lift my arm again. Former NFL coach Tony Dungy hit the nail on the head when he said, *"The first step toward creating an improved future is the ability to envision it."* That vision must be followed by venture.

Hope doesn't just land in your lap. Hope is created by envisioning and defining what it is that you're hoping for, and placing a value on that vision. What was it worth to me, and what was I willing to do to see what I hoped for happen? If I didn't have a deep down peace to believe that I could recover, there was no fuel to ignite my withered flame. I love what Proverbs says about this need for fuel: *"The human spirit can endure a sick body, but who can bear a crushed spirit?" Proverbs 18:14 (NLT).* My body was crushed, but my spirit was empowered by my Father in Heaven.

> *I was struggling enough that I was always on the verge of giving up and losing my drive, so I avoided any influence to do so.*

I discovered that hope and positive energy go hand in hand. I couldn't create or transfer positive energy on my own. I learned that choosing who I spent time with would matter more now than ever. If someone put off negative energy, I simply could not afford to be around them. I was struggling enough that I was always on the verge of giving up and losing my drive, so I avoided any influence to do so.

I also began to expose myself to the proper resources from an attitude and mindset standpoint. First and foremost, I dusted off my Bible and I found encouragement and direction every time I opened it. Before the avalanche, I read books in pursuit of knowledge, and continuously had one book going. When I finished, I would start another, mostly with leadership as the topic. Jim Rohn said it best when he said, *"All the information you need to succeed already exists. The problem is, you're not exposing yourself to it."*

In order to succeed in my situation, I exposed myself to information that applied to the struggles I was facing. You'll hear me a handful of times in this book use quotes by David Foster. He's become one of my biggest motivators as an author and speaker. I began to read his book THE POWER TO PREVAIL. I read it slowly and absorbed everything that I could. I would type and save in my phone, phrases and quotes that I could apply in my recovery and life. I've hung onto something that I read the very first day, on page three, in fact:

> *"God gave us a climbing gear and an ascending spirit in order to prepare us to prevail over adversity. He dropped us into this competitive, sometimes dark, always dangerous world, equipped to live as victors, not victims."*

Continuing on the Road to *Victory*

I was continuing to meet with a speech therapist as my speech was still affected by the brain injury. Within a few weeks, my therapist determined that my speech wasn't really being affected by a motor or mechanics problem, but instead at the brain itself; if I slowed down and thought it through, I could smoothly execute the routine.

I was given some exercises to use at home and discharged from speech therapy. Again it would become a challenge of the mind, a battle to constantly remind myself to think through what I was trying to speak. I was mentally exhausted by the end of each day as my balance, left leg motor, and speech were all tied to the brain injury and required constant thought processing in order to function.

It was very challenging at times. I could easily become a victim. The world could feel sorry for me for the rest of my life. "It's just so tough, this battle I fight, if you only knew what I go through every day." "The pain is tremendous." Whine, cry, poor me. Or NOT! The God inspired ability to instead be a *victor* allowed me to continue to inspire with my attitude in the midst of grim odds and an ugly long-term prognosis.

It wasn't until I settled into my at-home routine that I began to realize the true power of our human minds. Our bodies can't function without them. We take for granted all of the simple things we do each day that become second nature.

We walk, we talk, we chew, we touch, we grip—all without thinking twice about it. I was forced to even think through what I was chewing in my mouth in order to not swallow too soon and risk choking. Even with a cane, I was forced to place tremendous focus on balance to keep from falling down. I had to remember to command my left leg to step forward, or it would stay planted, drag, and trip me.

I was also finding that the world assumes that I have two hands. Many things required tremendous effort and thought, or at times proved impossible with only one. When I had left my world earlier that year, I was out of bed and on the go at 6 a.m., and didn't stop until it was bedtime again. I had taken my daily freedom and my two hands for granted—and I bet you do too. Now, I was viewing life through a different lens and learning to appreciate the small things that my old lens had filtered out.

It's Time

Early on in the at home recovery, I stopped Mary to tell her, "It's time."

"Time for what?"

I explained to her that I wanted to slide back into my black slacks and pressed white Toyota shirt and make an appearance at work.

Each Friday morning, all managers and salespeople would have our weekly sales meeting. I asked Mary if she would help me get dressed for the next Friday morning so I could surprise my crew. We ironed my clothes and slid them on. I got out of her car to slowly hobble in with my cane, a slinged up left arm, and battered body. The guys lit up when I walked inside and I was greeted by many of the crew.

The meeting was in the upstairs conference room, so a couple of the guys hung back to assist me up the stairs. The energy in the room was great and the atmosphere pushed the pain from the focal point to the background. I was asked to say a few words late in the meeting. As I spoke up, they heard a different voice than they had heard the last time I had directed the meeting—48 hours before my final ride. Although my speech was improving, the new Matt had a much softer tone and lower volume than the firm, clear voice they were accustomed to hearing before. My little pep talk on the 'little things' ended with a nice, warm, memorable applause from the crew.

More Change, New Tears

The new me was creating some tension on the home-front with Mary. The man she had known before rarely sat down, and now I was spending a good part of the day with my feet up. My emotions were operating at very immature levels and I would cry often in the evenings after a long day of physical and emotional pain. Each day was a battle for me and Mary began to allow it to put constant strain on her.

I'll never forget the argument in the bedroom that morning. The strain weighed too heavy and she voiced out firmly "I can't do this anymore!"

"Do what?" I replied, searching for more details.

She immediately said "Be your caretaker, and your girlfriend!"

My eyes filled with tears and I still remember the confusion in my mind. I had tried so hard not to be a weight. My dad had come to stay in town to help for a while and a good friend that I had worked with joined to trade off giving me rides to therapy and helping at the gym. I would even fight the pain to get up and help load the dishwasher or pick up the house. Caretaker?

Although confused, I felt a deep down peace that it was ok, that it was the right move for me to have a change in my living situation. And it was. I moved out three days later to J.W.'s basement, where my dad had been staying. My recovery was more productive and progressive without the stress of maintaining a difficult relationship under the same roof.

God knew what was best for me. Mary and I continued to grow apart and she eventually left my life. Even though it was best for both of us, it was extremely difficult to lose her. I had lost so much already and now I was losing the woman I loved. There were times I literally bawled my eyes out with a broken heart. However, I also began to learn again that tears would bring healing. I ran across an encouraging Native American proverb that takes it deep to say:

> *"The soul would have no rainbow if the eyes had no tears."*

The rehab schedule continued at an intense level. I was finally discharged from speech, cognitive, and occupational therapy after reaching satisfactory levels. My life now consisted of physical therapy, gym, walks around the neighbor-hood with my 'walking stick,' and sleep. I would soon start to see the repetition pay off, but for now it was enough to just "keep on keepin' on." I continued to attend the Friday meetings and spend a little time at work to give me contact with the outside world. I was even working partial days a couple of days a week. I had approached Ryan and his dad about working part-time for no salary, just as a method of therapy to help my mind heal and keep me active. I also discovered that keeping my mind occupied helped distract me from the constant, intense nerve pain.

Boundaries

I was finding out more daily that my world was so different. It was hard to find my place again. At times I felt completely overwhelmed and would tell myself "I can't do this. I can't keep up with life anymore." Looking back, I now realize the primary reason that feeling was so strong: boundaries. I was being forced to learn to set boundaries in my life, something I had needed to do for a long time, but hadn't done.

I had always been the guy who could handle it all. "Sure, I can take care of that. No problem, I can work late tonight. You bet, come over for dinner tonight. Oh ya, the snow is great, I can run to Canada to film this weekend." I always made the excuse, "That's just my personality type. I'm an on-the-go kind of guy."

*Examine your life. Are you exhausted? Is it costing you or your family? If so, make it a part of your life to **choose not** to follow in my footsteps.*

The truth was, I had a complete inability to set boundaries. In reality, that inability is what cost me my family. Even when I did make time for my wife and kids, I was exhausted, both physically and emotionally. I convinced myself that it was just part of life. It is 'just part of life,' but only in relation to the *choice* that has to be made.

Stop reading for a minute, lay this book down. Examine your life. Are you exhausted? Is it costing you or your family? If so, make it part of your life to *choose not* to follow in my footsteps.

I also came to the realization about identity, that I mentioned previously: I believe that many times, we make the mistake of wrapping our identity up in the "stuff" in life; in the things we do, not in *who* we are. We run so much deeper than what we do in this life. There is just so much more to *who* we are than *what* we are.

What if all I knew myself to be was a talented snowmobiler and a productive businessman? I was put in a situation where I could no longer be either for a season of life, maybe longer. Nevertheless, I was still Matt and *that* was worth fighting for. A man of integrity, a sense of humor, deep personality, loving and caring, motivated—all of these have so much more value than the title, "Extreme Snowmobiler."

In twelve seconds, I lost the ability to ride a snowmobile. Short of losing my life, you can't take any of the rest of that away from me. There's a lot more to Matt Potratz than what you saw on your television or read in a magazine.

In The Storm

Fighting through a storm of this magnitude can't realistically produce only happy, inspirational stories. Getting pummeled by life's wind and waves is bound to produce some very low times. When energy, emotion, drive, motivation, and passion are all running on empty, it nearly brings life to a halt, literally. Suffering through debilitating nerve pain 24 hours a day on top of fighting physical injuries, all the while trying to find my place in my world again, knocked the wind out of my sail.

There were times I would ask God, "Please let me go to sleep in peace and not wake up. Rescue me from this pain and take me to heaven." I was serious! I would cry myself to sleep many nights as I was just so exhausted from the fight. It's scary even to write it, as one night my story nearly ended.

I was stirred from my sleep at 2 a.m. by some pulsating nerve pain that would sometimes shoot up my arm. I had experienced the same pulsations at work a time or two and I had to go outside to my truck and cry my way through it. This time, I was running on empty. I felt I had fought a good fight but could fight no more.

In tears, I got up to drag my snowmobile gear bag out of the closet. I began to slowly pull my pants on with my one hand. I decided to dress in all my riding gear, head to toe, go to the nearby bridge over the Snake River, put on the helmet that I had worn in the avalanche, and jump off. My thought was that God didn't get the job done right the first time so I would gear up and finish it. Instead, God showed Himself to be real and loving.

As I finished my pants and sat down on the bed to put on my jersey, God halted the train! He swept into my mind memories of a recent event. My boy

Ethan was very close to his grandparents' black lab and she had passed away. It crushed him. His doggy was gone. His mom or myself would at times find him crying and when asked what was wrong, he would reply, "Sadie's gone forever and she's not gonna come back." I assured him that she was in heaven, but in tears he said, "But I don't want her to be in heaven, I want her to be here with me."

It hit me with twice the force of the avalanche! God clearly spoke these words: "Matt, his doggy is gone and he is crushed. What if his daddy was gone?" The tears rushed down my face as I dropped the jersey and laid back on the bed.

I immediately erased my plan from the drawing board. Now, it wasn't even an option. Taking my life would be an extremely selfish move. Sure, it would deliver me from my pain, but leave my boys with a lifetime of pain, missing their daddy. The pain of losing his doggy was passing pretty quickly, but the pain of losing his daddy would leave a void that could never be sufficiently filled. God went straight to my heart to get my attention. He knew it was powerful enough to stop me not dead, but alive in my tracks. That was the last time I ever considered that selfish action! When your mind leads you astray, dig deep and your heart will find the way.

> *Sure, it would deliver me from the pain, but leave my boys with a lifetime of pain, missing their daddy.*

I also struggled with blaming God. I think we all do at some point in our lives. But, I began to understand that God hadn't made the avalanche happen, I made it happen. He allowed it to happen, but the freedom of choice we've had since Adam and Eve gave me the option to put myself in that situation. Often that freedom puts us into some sticky situations because we're, well, human.

Understanding that He hadn't made this happen and experiencing His power and love in the midst of my struggles made me learn to praise him, regardless of how severely the storm raged around me. I hung on to a song by "Casting Crowns," that carries a beautiful message: *"Praise You In This Storm."*

I want to share those lyrics with you. They may find you in a storm of life or a stormy season of your life. These are the words I would sing:

I was sure by now
God, You would have reached down
And wiped our tears away
Stepped in and saved the day
But once again, I say "Amen,"
And it's still raining

As the thunder rolls
I barely hear Your whisper
   through the rain
"I'm with you"
And as Your mercy falls
I raise my hands and praise the God
Who gives and takes away

And I'll praise You in this storm
And I will lift my hands
For You are who You are
No matter where I am
And every tear I've cried
You hold in Your hand
You never left my side
And though my heart is torn
I will praise You in this storm

I remember when
I stumbled in the wind
You heard my cry to you
And you raised me up again
My strength is almost gone
How can I carry on
If I can't find You

from PRAISE YOU IN THIS STORM, *by Casting Crowns*

"Praise the God who gives and takes away." It's easy to praise God, give thanks, and be happy when the sun is out. You'll find strength and peace that you never knew existed when you stop blaming Him, stop cursing Him, and choose to praise Him through your storm.

Hurricane Katrina literally shook our nation as it turned thousands of lives upside down. Think about this; how much more does a Katrina victim appreciate the sunshine after battling through that massive storm? We take life's sunshiny days for granted. We don't appreciate them. The storm gives us a new perspective—if we allow it to.

Embrace your storms! When they toss you, turn you, stretch you, soak you, let it wash you clean. When the clouds lift, you'll see your sunshine through a new set of eyes.

Behind New Walls

I settled into a routine, a lifestyle consumed by recovery. I was home but had an entirely new way of life; the same routine of exercise, therapy, and rest every day. I had trained my guys at work to process every car transaction the same, as every customer deserved to have the same experience. I learned to apply that same discipline to my routine, to process every day the same, give it all that I had.

The foundation of Tony Dungy's football program was, *"Do what we do, whatever it takes, no excuses, no explanations."* I simply couldn't afford to make excuses for all the reasons why I couldn't do the same routine over and over again. Life left me with the same choice that I had faced since awakening from my coma: do it now, or regret it later.

I was still fighting the idea of *wait and see*, and I just couldn't settle with it. My index finger could move just slightly, otherwise I'd had a completely dead left arm for nearly five months! My shoulder was starting to regain some strength but it was weak enough that the left side of my body basically just hung there. As I said, hope had become a critical part of my recovery and I needed some hope that there was reason to keep my arm.

We discussed the possibility of amputation but it was difficult to even talk about it. My dad and I began to do some internet research on the injury. We discovered a handful of similar injuries. Many of you know of the Mayo Clinic with a handful of locations in the nation. I had never heard of them, but it appeared to be our best contact. In Rochester, Minnesota was the team of hand and arm specialists.

Our initial phone conversation with a description of the injury and time frame confirmed that *wait and see* was not going to produce results. They instead wanted to evaluate me as soon as possible because they could possibly repair the damaged nerves. But if too much time passed, the nerves become unuseable, essentially dead in some cases.

I scheduled an appointment for a few weeks later and purchased my airline tickets. There was a sense of excitement just hearing that they were somewhat familiar with my injury and we were finally hoping to do something about it! Up until now, there had been nothing but uncertainty without any specific diagnosis. I had arrived home from my three month hospital stay a couple of months prior. Now I was headed back inside some new walls—this time with a new drive and purpose.

– 6 –

NEW WALLS

"Our eyes are placed in the front of our heads for a reason; to look forward, not back."

(Unknown)

WHEN MY DAD AND I GOT ON THE PLANE, CONVERSATION WAS SOMEWHAT LIMITED AS I CONTINUED TO REFLECT BACK ON THE EXPERIENCE THAT HAD LEFT ME WITH A HANGING LEFT ARM. The flight was also a reminder of the increase in the nerve pain intensity brought on by altitude; this time, a much longer flight from Lewiston to Salt Lake City then on to Minneapolis.

We touched down safely and prepared for our final leg. With two tall Potratz guys and our gear packed in a little rental car, we arrived in Rochester. We had made arrangements to stay at the Nazarene Well House to save on the cost of the trip as the financial strain over the nearly six months down was significant.

We also made plans to meet up with one of my sponsors, Ray Schoenfelder, owner of Black Diamond Xtreme Engineering (located near Rochester). It was excellent to meet in person as our interaction had been all by phone or e-mail. My idea of a "clinic" had been a relatively small facility and organization. That mentality changed quickly August 4, 2009 when we rolled into downtown Rochester to see three fifteen-plus story buildings—all Mayo clinic. It also seemed as if there was a Mayo building of some kind on nearly every street corner.

I felt the sensation of the syringe being pushed and sliding thru to my spinal cord. I could even feel the dye entering my body.

I was scheduled for a few tests, then to meet with the "Brachial Plexus" team for a discussion of my situation. The brachial plexus is a group of nerves in the armpit area that are the command center for arm operation. Essentially, five main nerves come out of the spinal cord and route through the brachial plexus, where they branch out to a bunch of smaller nerves to activate the many different movements of the arm.

My medical records had already been sent to the team so they were familiar with my case. As I shook hands with the team of doctors, it already felt as if I was in the right place. It was encouraging to finally talk with someone who had extensive knowledge on the issue, something I hadn't had up to this point. I was honored even to meet them; three of the best neurosurgeons in the world. Their knowledge was apparent within just a few minutes of discussion.

Although severe brachial plexus damage was a rare injury, the team stayed busy as people came from all over the nation to seek help. They explained that they expected damage to one or more of the five main nerves that feed the brachial plexus, and even a good possibility of nerve root avulsion at the cord. A series of tests and scans would tell us the story.

I had been through some rigorous tests, scans, and procedures, but little did I know that this day would hold the most difficult one yet. In the MRI, they were unable to get an accurate look at the damaged nerves that were hanging from the spinal cord. The fluid in the nerves shows up clear and blends in producing a vague image. They needed to inject dye into the nerves to give them some color, but you can't inject directly into the nerves. Instead, they needed to inject the dye into my spinal cord and direct it toward the nerves to fill the core and give them color on the scan.

This is where the fun stopped. I was first placed face down and strapped to a stainless steel table, which was very uncomfortable in my physical condition. My lower back was numbed to make way for the large needle to inject the dye. Although I felt no pain, I felt the sensation of the syringe being pushed and sliding thru to my spinal cord. I could even feel the dye entering my body. As I write this it's been 18 months since the procedure and I still cringe with detailed memory every time I think of it.

After the dye was fully injected, it was time to direct it from the bottom of my back to the damaged nerves near my neck. Gravity was their tool of choice to get the job done. The electronic table was raised at the feet until I was nearly directly head down, feet up so the dye could run down, or in this case, up the cord to the injury. As I'm positive you can imagine, hanging head first with my shoulders against braces waiting for this to take place was about as comfortable as sitting down for an afternoon stroll on a bicycle without a seat, with the seat post still in place! Then, it was back to the tube for a new scan.

The story was not what we had hoped for. The series of scans had shown severe brachial plexus damage. Of the five nerves, two were broke in half, two were literally avulsed from the spinal cord, and one hanging on by a thread. They thought there was a possibility that a couple of them may be repairable but the damage was significant. They had also discovered that because so much time had gone by with no nerve activity in my arm, my bicep muscle had atrophied to the point that it would no longer be useable to lift my arm.

"So, what's the option, amputation?" I said in a sad and probably scared voice. "I've got no nerves and no muscle."

"No," the doctor confidently replied. "All that being said, we still have a plan. We will first harvest a muscle from the inside of your right thigh called the *gracilis* and transplant it to your bicep area. This muscle is harvested relatively often to assist in knee replacements and other things of that nature. You will most likely not even know it's gone unless you plan to undergo strenuous athletic activity."

"Then," he continued, "to give that muscle the nerve actuation it needs, we believe we can borrow intercostal nerves from your chest. These nerves activate the muscles that inhale and exhale. We'll do some tests to confirm, but we believe your breathing will be healthy and efficient enough to spare three of these nerves with little or no effect on your breathing. We'll detach the nerves but leave them live, and re-route them to your bicep area to be attached to the gracilis. We hope to move sensory fibers and motor fibers to give you minimal, but some sensation along with motor function. If it's all successful, in time we hope to see roughly thirty to forty percent arm use back, with at least the ability to lift your arm."

> *I remember saying a thank you prayer right then for those millimeters. I was millimeters away from taking my boys for wheelchair rides instead of walks.*

Too Close For Comfort

They then made a request I wasn't expecting. Dr. Bishop spoke up and said "Matt, would you stand up and walk across the room for us?" I did so a couple of times at their request and he said "Wow, we are just surprised how well you walk; pretty fluid motion."

They proceeded to pull the scan of my spinal cord up on the screen and said "Matt, even if none of this arm stuff works, you are still one lucky man." They showed me my crushed vertebrae on the screen. "Where these were crushed down, if the vertebrae had touched here," he said as he pointed at the screen, "you would have been paralyzed from the waist down. The gap is millimeters. Millimeters are too close for comfort in our line of work. You're fine now because your spine has been stabilized and fused, but it was a close call."

I remember saying a 'thank you' prayer right then for those millimeters. I was millimeters away from taking my boys for wheelchair rides instead of walks.

Nothing was said about the awful nerve pain I had been enduring so I brought up the subject. They said the surgery would do nothing for the pain and my heart sunk.

"Here's the problem we're facing," the doctor went on to say. "Although the hand hurts tremendously, the pain isn't coming from your hand. The brain is getting a false signal from the spinal cord with the message that the hand hurts. The injury, the damage, is at the spinal cord, not the lower extremity. We call this 'phantom' nerve pain."

"So what are my options?" I asked.

"Basically, just long term medication." I immediately had a knot in my stomach. I was taking a significant daily dose of Lyrica, Hydrocodone, and even Oxycontin to cope with the pain. I hated the medication! Drowsiness, foggy mind, weird emotions, just to name a few—every day! The wind had been knocked out of my sail. I thought for sure they would be able to help with the pain if they could fix my arm.

"Are you sure?" I replied. "I can live with one arm. I can't live with this pain. I would love to be able to use this arm again but I would give that up in a heart-beat to have the pain go away."

"Well, there are some options out there. They are relatively new procedures so we really can't make a recommendation. The repair has to take place at the cord so there's plenty of risk involved. It's nothing that we do here."

There wasn't really a lot of risk involved in this motor nerve transplant surgery because they would be operating on a limb that was already motionless so I quickly made the decision to proceed. I knew that something had to be done.

They went on to tell me that in order to harvest the nerves from my chest cavity, a breathing test would first be done to make sure my inhaling was healthy enough to spare a few nerves. We scheduled that test and a few others that were needed to prepare for surgery.

They sent me to meet with a pain consultant on site for proper medication dosage and ideas to deal with the pain. I honestly don't remember a word he said. I had so much on my mind with the surgery and the news about the pain that I was in a zone.

As we settled back in at the Well House, it was difficult for me to process the prognosis on the intense nerve pain. I had been training myself not to think about the pain and keep my mind on other things. I didn't even talk about the pain. You rarely, if ever, heard me say, "My hand hurts so bad" or "This sucks!" or "I wish I didn't have to deal with this," nothing like that. I had learned that the more I thought about it, the worse it hurt. Back in Lewiston, my pain doctor and I had discussed that "All pain comes from the brain." If the tip of your finger hurts, the signal goes from the finger to the spinal cord to the brain, every time. So the pain control center is the mind.

Learning to isolate the pain thoughts and minimize them had become my best defense. My hand hurt worse that night than it had in a long time because it consumed my mind. We had promised all of our friends on Caring Bridge an update so my dad posted an update in the Journal. A few tears dripped down my cheeks as I went to sleep and my dad stayed up to type these words:

> "Today was a difficult day to say the least. We had to be at the hospital for an MRI at 6:00 am (that translates to 4:00 am PST!) followed by an EMG (a very painful nerve test) at 8:15 am and then the consultation with the Brachial Plexus Nerve Surgical Team at 2:00 pm.

> "The real difficulty came as a result of the consultation as they painted a rather bleak picture for us regarding any repairs to the damaged nerves. Without going into a lot of details, suffice it to say that the damaged nerves are not repairable as they were actually torn loose (avulsed) from the spinal cord leaving a lot of scar tissue and trapped blood at the site of the avulsion.

> "The damaged spot on the spinal cord is sending the messages of pain to the brain and there are few methods available other than medication to treat this type of pain. That news was a bit devastating for Matt as he was hoping to get some relief from the pain while we were here.

> "The upside to the consultation is that there are some surgical procedures that could allow Matt to get some control and movement back in his shoulder and elbow thus allowing him to rid himself of the arm sling. This surgery is a pretty extensive procedure with a 75% success rate. The surgery will be performed in mid-September here at the Mayo Clinic.

> "All of this translates into a further need to pray and continue to ask God for a miracle. We've all seen God do miraculous things in Matt's recovery and relief for the pain would be one more step in that process. He is resolved to the fact that he may never get full use of the arm back but is struggling with the thought of living with daily pain for the rest of his life.

"We will be traveling back home later in the week after a few more tests and one more consultation. Feel free to keep those cards, letters and emails coming as they have been a real source of encouragement to Matt."

When we woke in the morning, we had already received a handful of comments back on Caring Bridge encouraging me and offering up prayer. I felt compelled to write a personal message to my friends to let them know where I stood after the news; to let them hear it from my mouth, from my heart—something I hadn't done much of up to this point. I told my dad and he agreed. I sat down to write it out to them over morning coffee. My dad typed for me as I spoke these words:

"Even though the news from yesterday was hard to take and certainly pretty disappointing, I wanted to write a personal note to let all of you know where I stand in the face of this difficulty. I made some tough decisions in my own heart and mind today as I faced the reality of long-term chronic pain and decided that I am not going to give up!

*"As my sales trainer Dan Culver taught me, and I always say; "**Focus on the things you CAN change.**" While I can't change what has happened to me, I CAN change how I respond to it. I am still going to be the Matt Potratz that all of you know. I am still going to be a great father to my kids, and for sure, be the friend to all of you that I've always been.*

"Most importantly, I want to be a voice for the God who obviously saved my life for a reason. Thanks for all of your support and prayers over the past five months and your continued prayers as we face the next steps in my recovery."

12 Hours

We went back to the Mayo to finish up the pre-op testing and made arrangements to fly home. I arrived home and went right back to work hoping the month would pass quickly so that we could get on with the surgery and one step closer to a functioning left arm. Time did pass quickly but I remember at times daydreaming of the hope of using my arm again. The recovery battle had put enough on my plate that I didn't dwell on my paralyzed limb but the nerve pain was always a reminder that it was there, therefore a reminder that it didn't function. I had faced nothing but uncertainty and *wait and see* up to this point and it often got pushed to the wayside.

It was encouraging and exciting to finally have my dead arm in the crosshairs and in the focus of some of the best surgeons in the nation. My Dad needed to fill obligations at work, and I could have made the flight alone, but many things were difficult for me including handling my luggage. Ryan Rogers stepped up to the plate and made arrangements to leave the dealership for a couple of days to fly me back out there.

When we arrived at the airport in Minneapolis, we had some downtime. "Potratz," Ryan said, "After all this, we need to get you a massage." So we did just that. I'd never even been to a massage parlor or massage therapist so my first time was going to be an airport massage parlor.

I told Ryan, "We should hang a sign around my neck that says 'Fragile. Handle with care.'" It was actually pretty painful but it was just the ticket to relieve some tension.

I contacted Ray from Black Diamond again and set up dinner so he and Ryan could meet. At dinner Ray told Ryan the story of his own near-death experience in an avalanche, a story he had previously told me. Ray also gives thanks to God for his survival. His had occurred before avalanche beacons were a common safety item for backcountry sledders. As you can imagine, the story shook me up as any avalanche story still does today.

The next morning we arrived at the Mayo Clinic bright and early to prepare for the lengthy and complex surgery. They informed me on the basics of the procedure. They would open me up to gain access to the damaged nerves and at that time, determine if the nerves were repairable. The condition of existing nerves would determine the quantity of intercostal nerves to be transplanted from my chest. They would make a decision mid-surgery whether the existing arm nerves could still be strong enough for arm function or if it would require the transplanted nerves to get the job done.

They estimated that the gracilis muscle transplant and the nerve transplant together would take about ten hours. Yes, that's ten hours in surgery! The team of three would do the operation together with their support teams in the room as well. They explained that they would not proceed with any decisions, such as the condition of the nerves, unless all three surgeons agreed on the matter. They also explained that there was little, but some risk involved in being sedated for so many hours. That's the last thing I remember before fading out for my nice long nap.

First on the agenda was to remove the gracilis muscle from my right thigh and prepare it for transplant to my arm. Apparently, a muscle gets its blood supply and oxygen through the skin. So, to keep the muscle alive during transplant, it was necessary to also remove a piece of skin from my thigh to take with the muscle. That skin would stay with the muscle and therefore be grafted on my upper bicep. Then they accessed the nerves and all agreed that even repaired, would not be strong enough to activate the arm.

The intercostal nerves from my rib cage were detached, left live, and rerouted to be attached to my new bicep: the gracilis muscle. The surgery was completed at about the eleventh hour mark and I remained out for another hour or so, for a total of twelve hours. As I came around, I quickly learned that in order for the skin graft to take properly, the room temperature would need to remain at 80° to 85° for about 36 hours. The thermostat was set at a balmy 85°. I don't think that takes much explanation, as I'm sure you can imagine: not comfortable!

Once it was confirmed that the operation was without complication, Ryan made arrangements to fly home and my dad would fly out a few days later to fly me home. Before discharge I received some instructions on the new therapy and rehab needed. My first instruction was simply to do a heavy breathing routine each day to fire the muscles that inhale and exhale. By firing those muscles, I was firing the transplanted nerves and keeping them active. Although they were now in my arm, my brain assumed they were still breathing, and over time, we could retrain the brain to use them for arm function. But, the first task at hand was to fire them daily to prevent them from becoming inactive.

I was also instructed and warned that I had a lifetime limitation on range of motion. Even today, if my arm goes above shoulder height, above a 90 degree angle, it will most likely tear the transplanted nerves and a $140,000 surgery and plenty of rehab goes down the road. Note to self: don't let arm go above shoulder!

Another Course in Patience

Flying home was interesting because in order for the new nerves to take properly and heal, my elbow was at a 90 from my abdomen and my arm was in a sling on a big pad pointed straight out from my body. They found us a proper seat, and onward to Idaho we went. I was told to lay low for four to five weeks to rest and recover. I needed a little assistance initially but I quickly got used to my new setup and got back out and about.

The most difficult part was learning to sleep on my back, elbow bent, and my arm pointed straight up because I couldn't remove the restraint. Staying clean meant a sponge bath in my shower chair. A little over a week went by and I'd had enough laying low. I figured a week was close enough to four or five so I found a way to get in my black slacks and white pressed shirt and went back to work. My new sling was black so I was even color coordinated. I looked more like a traffic cop giving signals with my arm sticking straight forward, but I figured I could pass as a sales manager.

My arm that had been cradled in a sling by my side was now the center of attention, literally! The reason for the continuous restraint on arm movement was to give those nerves time to find their place and start to essentially take root. This took time, and time meant hassle and discomfort. I was forced to exercise more of the patience I had learned thus far in my fight. I got out of bed early each morning to give myself the time it took to improvise around my healing arm.

> *I looked more like a traffic cop giving signals with my arm sticking straight forward, but I figured I could pass as a sales manager.*

I recently met a new friend who goes by "Lefty." He suffered the same brachial plexus injury in a motorcycle accident. His was severe enough that he chose amputation. Lefty now guides snowmobile trips in the incredible mountains outside of Togwotee, Wyoming. He has learned to improvise and adapt, and ride very well with one arm. One day, he said these words to me:

> *"Improvise, Adapt, and Overcome. Seemed fitting to me as a marine. As an amputee, it's a way of life."*

Long Term Medication

The one statement from the Mayo Clinic that kept running through my mind was, "Basically, just long term medication." I had a deep desire to be med-free. That desire burned in me daily. I, of course, appreciated some pain relief, but I hated the way that the meds made me feel. One night, I capitalized on that burning desire. Oxycontin was probably my most effective medication for pain, but unfortunately the most affective on my mood, attitude, thought processing, etc., as well. That evening, I was in a small argument with Mary's brother about how our relationship had ended. At one point, he said something along the lines of: "You're an addict, and you don't even know it."

"I have a better handle on it than you realize," I fired back. "In fact, I'm going to start eliminating meds, starting with oxy!"

He actually laughed a little and assured me that, "Brother, you'll *never* get off oxy on your own. You'll end up in rehab. That stuff is intense!"

That was exactly what I needed to hear: "You'll *never* get off…" I skipped my night-time dose that night and the battle started. I wasn't doing it to prove him wrong, I was doing it to improve my life. I had no idea what I was about to face. My body had become accustomed to regular intake of a powerful drug, and I took it away, cold turkey. My body let me know what it thought about that decision.

When I woke to my alarm the next morning, I could already feel the increase in pain and my body's desire to take that morning dose. I texted work with what I was up to, skipped that morning dose, ate a small breakfast, and went right back to bed. As the day wore on, my body began to slowly, but surely, go into a panic for more of that chemical. I was very tempted to head for the medicine cabinet. But, I held back.

That evening, I shook with chills. My body felt ice cold. I piled the blankets on in bed to warm up. Then it shifted and I had sweat pouring down my face. I remember thinking, "Wow, so this is what it's like to recover from drug addiction." It gave me a new respect for those that do so.

At one point, I felt to be at my breaking point, I had to make it stop. I headed for the med cabinet and talked to God as I walked. I didn't want to start over. "God, give me the strength." I decided I could do a small dose and get by. I poured the pill on the counter, but then I stopped. I felt a similar assurance I had felt many times in the hospital. I put the pill back in the bottle, went back to bed, curled up tight and God let me rest, I fell asleep. I woke in the night to use the bathroom, but was able to fight back to sleep.

The next morning, I again notified work that I wouldn't be there, filled up my big water bottle and drank a ton of H2O as I fought the sickness. The symptoms were similar, yet milder off and on through the day and again the next day. I ate decent portions that third day and again drank a ton of water.

Day four, I woke up still feeling a little sick, but got dressed and went to work. I smiled a little as the thought, "You'll *never* get off" ran through my head again.

Of course, I recommend that you don't duplicate my stubbornness. Follow your doctor's orders and taper your dose if you are eliminating meds. I was only on a medium dosage, but my doctor informed me that quitting 'cold turkey' when on a high enough dose can actually cause your body to go into shock. Fortunately, with God's help I was instead able to leave that man who said "never" in *shock*.

– 7 –
THROUGH A NEW LENS

"Be grateful for what you've been given, not hateful for what you've lost."

David Foster

A FEW MONTHS FOLLOWING THE MAYO CLINIC, NEW YEARS PLANS WERE MADE TO HEAD FOR RYAN'S CABIN. I hadn't really spoken much about it but was wrestling with an idea; was it time to get back on the seat? I felt that it was. Initially my friends said, "No way, not yet!" When word spread through the building at work, it caused a bit of a stir and I got a few lectures. I sought the approval and advice of one of my closest friends. I phoned my Dad.

His thoughts were, "Matt, it might be too soon, it's not even been a year. But you know your body better than anyone and I know this would be a much needed victory for your heart and mind. So if you're ready, then I say go for it. What machine are you riding?"

I said "Dad, it's out of the shop and fully repaired, I have to ride my turbo sled again."

There was excitement to go for it coupled with stirred emotions. First, I had to make a modification. The throttle is operated with the right hand, but the brake is operated with the left. I joked that I was going to have to learn to use my brakes for the first time! Before, I had been unaware of any need to slow down. "Little black trigger on the right, mash it!"

I contacted Ray from Black Diamond Engineering, the sponsor and friend I spent time with while at Mayo Clinic. As always, Ray said, "No problem," put a right handed brake setup together and priority shipped it to Idaho. Brake and throttle would be operated by the same hand: let off one trigger, get on the other. You never operate brake and throttle at the same time so Ray was right, "No problem!" Loading the same snowmobile back on the trailer that I nearly lost my life aboard, was victorious, but nerving at the same time. I had some help but I insisted on being the one to ride it up the ramp and onto the trailer. Even when loaded and ready, my friends still challenged me a little, but I stood firm as I knew deep down that I needed it. I had lost enough, I needed a win.

The primary reason that I wanted to ride from Ryan's cabin was because it's located in McCall. I felt that it was even more of a victory to get back on the seat in my favorite riding area: the mountain range that nearly took my life. First, we had to see if I could even ride at all in my condition.

The drive down brought on a weird, but good feeling. I borrowed a truck from work, a trailer from a friend and made the road trip alone. I'm a strong person, but I have to admit that there was some doubt. I wrestled with the plan on my three hour drive.

At the cabin, the group warmed me with an awesome welcome. We celebrated the New Year that night with friends and fellow riders. My one-armed maiden voyage that was set for the next morning came up in conversation a handful of times. "Are you sure?" were three words that came up more than once.

I was sure. January 1, 2010 was ten months to the day from the day that changed my life forever. Early reports in my coma and recovery left my family not even considering that I would get back on a snowmobile, they were considering the possibility that I may not ever live at home without full-time assistance. At one point in the hospital, I spoke clearly to Jon, "I will never ride a snowmobile ever again!" As I healed, I developed a deep desire to defeat that fear. I somehow knew that it was a necessary piece in my recovery puzzle.

Defeat Fear

I woke up the next morning full of energy! As I finished breakfast and started to gear up, Ryan stopped me to say, "Potratz, you don't have to do this. Are you sure you're okay to ride?"

"Ryan," I assured him, "I'll take it slow and easy but I have to do this."

We laughed together as he said, "I don't know what to do with you sometimes."

I crawled aboard my sled and closed my eyes to pray. When I opened my eyes I looked at my instruments and gauges. I remembered that my turbo control box for EFI fuel control also had a "stats" mode and it would record peak boost. I scrolled to thru the stats to see that when the avalanche broke loose ten months earlier and my track fought to keep clawing, I peaked at a max turbo boost of 10.4 pounds cranking the engine to a speed of 7,950 rpm.

That may not mean much to you but it was all part of looking back to reflect on that day one last time, and move forward. I certainly wasn't going to reach those engine performance levels on this day. My primary focus was what it had never been before: *don't fall off.* (It's okay to laugh, I did as I wrote it.)

When I was riding at the elite level, I rarely stopped to appreciate the breeze in my face or the beauty of the snow on the pine trees. I was focused on loosening up, and being fluid, and warming up my machine, and a route to take, what chutes to climb, and, and, and...

Today was different! I took off down the trail and got a good feel for balance with a weak core and one arm. I rode pretty smoothly down the trail with no difficulties. The group stopped shortly into the ride to check on my comfort level. I removed my goggles before continuing, for one reason; to feel the fresh air touch the skin on my face. At that moment my body was in significant pain but my soul could have melted the snow! I did it! Much of my fight had been with this day on the radar!

I went until I was struggling to hang on and turned back. I rolled back onto my trailer as the trip meter rolled to 16.2 miles. I was in pain but smiling and celebrating inside! The most painful 16 miles I've ever ridden became the most rewarding miles out of my nearly 20,000 miles on the seat of a snowmobile.

Something else significant happened to start my new year. I made the choice to slide back into a full time schedule at work. The doctors' forecast had looked quite stormy as it appeared that my mental capacity would be such that I wouldn't be able to carry out the responsibilities of a normal job, or a normal life for that matter.

They had also painted a picture that prepared us for the fact that my physical condition would likely limit me greatly, hence it was unlikely that I would ever crawl back behind the handlebars of a snowmobile. Now, just ten months, to the day, from ground zero, I was well on the road to doing all three again! In the doctors' defense, they hadn't taken into consideration that God didn't just do miracles back in the days when the Bible was written, He is still in the miracle business in the 21st century!

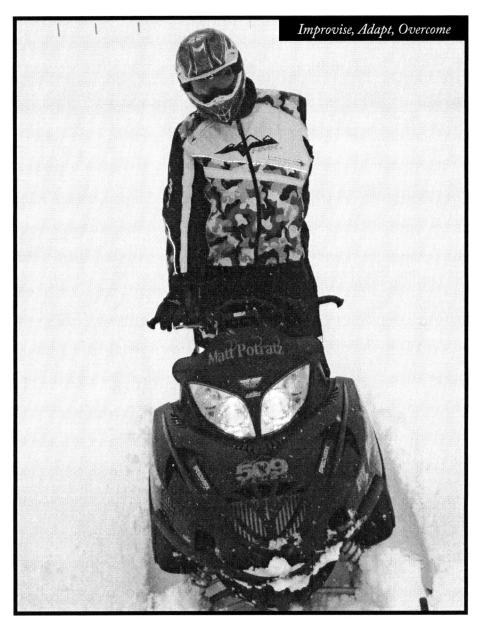

I rode a couple of more short rides in the next couple of months and began feeling more comfortable and stronger. March 1st rolled around, my one year mark. There would be no riding today. On this March 1st, I took the day off of work and celebrated with my boys. My primary motivation during those twelve months was certainly not to get back on a snowmobile or to get back to work. No, it was to be able to raise three boys to be young men of integrity; to be dad again!

The following weekend was a different story, a new victory to celebrate. It was time. I contacted Phil, the film producer from 208 and asked if he cared to join me to make the trip back to the avalanche site. He agreed as did a few friends and we set the date. March 7, 2010, twelve months and six days after my life slid out, we were going back.

I veered off the trail to go cross country to the site and felt pretty good. Within minutes I broke over the hill for the view of my mountain. I knew where I wanted to stop to look straight at the chute; the same place I had left from to climb the mountain twelve long months earlier. It was literally spiritual! I sat there completely overwhelmed with appreciation!

As I scanned down a path of descent that I should never have survived, I appreciated God for saving my life. It stirred up mind pictures of ground zero, and I had sincere appreciation for those there that did everything right to rescue me. I thought about my path of recovery from hospitals to physical therapy, to work, to riding again. I was wearing the same goggles, but now viewing life through a completely different lens.

Phil and I discussed that we should do a dialogue on camera, so with the avalanche site in the background, I told fans and viewers what it felt like to be back. Another desire stirred up in me; to get back on the hill. Even if only a couple hundred feet up, I needed to complete today's journey.

> *I was wearing the same goggles, but now viewing life through a completely different lens.*

With camera rolling, one hand at the controls, I lined up and climbed the base of the hill to the mouth of the rock chute I had rocketed up seconds before the snow fractured. This day, I turned out of it and coasted quickly back off the mountain. My gut untied itself from the knot it was in as I rolled back to the group and shut my machine down for hugs and handshakes.

The following fall, viewers watched the special section of my dialogue and ascent in the extras of the sled film MOMENTUM. The original footage of the avalanche itself was in the film A CALCULATED RISK. For this day's ride back to the crash site, all reports calculated little or no risk of slides. I miscalculated on March 1st, 2009—but on March 7th, 2010, I defeated my fear and gained "momentum" to keep living the life that God has given me back.

Partially climbing the avalanche hill with one arm

I've taken a lot of ridicule for getting back on the seat. People would say, "How can you almost lose your life, go through that much pain and suffering, and still want to go again?" I look at it differently. I've always believed that when life gets you down, which it will, get up, get back on the horse, and go again.

You'll remember at one point early in the hospital stay, I did say that I would never ride again. The desire to do so continued to deepen as my recovery continued and I realized that my journey would never be complete until I felt the victory of defeating that fear. *"A bend in the road is not the end of the road, unless you fail to make the turn." (UNKNOWN)* I did do it partially to inspire fans and fellow riders, but most of all, I did it for Matt. My heart and mind needed a win. I needed to know I was getting my life back. *What will you do if life slides out?*

It Happened

In most spinal injuries, you can expect a little regression at some point. I pretty much remained on a steady ascent and even though I was aware that I could face a potential setback, I didn't realize how hard it would hit me. I had experienced some idle time when healing from surgeries, but never really gone backwards. Then it happened.

One morning the following winter, I woke to my right hand, my good hand, feeling weak and somewhat uncoordinated. I first noticed that I would struggle to open an envelope or to pick up something heavy that required a grip hold. Over the next week it began to become very difficult to button my pants, put on my socks and shoes, twist caps and knobs, all things that had become a simple task even with one hand.

I was frustrated, but I just kept praying and trying to remain positive, thinking that this is only a short-lived setback. I had ridden snowmobiles a few times that winter aboard my new sled, well kind of new, and with significantly less horsepower and weight. The machine was one I had sold a few years earlier, my Arctic Cat M7, the sled I was aboard the first time I ever rode for a camera. I was asked to help with a snowmobile fun run where the local club would have a marked route with checkpoints, prizes, and burgers on the grill.

I was going to help at one of the stops, where I would ride my machine out to the location to help with drawings and visit with riders. Even with the recent weakness, I decided I would be okay to participate. I struggled to pull the rope to start my snowmobile as the compression of the engine threatened to pull the handle loose from my weak grip. I was able to get it started and safely hang on to operate the throttle, the brake, to steer, and I made it through the day.

Over the next couple of weeks, the regression presented its challenges. At times my hand would feel okay; other times it was very weak. I had reached the point that I held water bottles between my knees and twisted the cap off easily with my hand but now I found myself opening a bottle of water with my teeth as my hand wasn't able to twist off the cap. I held back my frustration and tears when I couldn't pull my boys through the snow in their wagon because I couldn't keep ahold of the handle with their weight in tow.

My left leg also started randomly flaring up with spasms in a stomping motion and when I rode the bike at the gym, it would do the same. I had a checkup with my pain doctor and decided to bounce the symptoms off of him as he had a lot of knowledge regarding spinal injuries. He explained that some regression is normal, but wasn't sure as to the root of the problem. He scheduled an E.M.G. for the next week to narrow down the problem at the neurological level. I was familiar with the test, as you may remember; I had gone through a few of the same procedures to check nerve activity in my left arm.

My brother called and was coming up from Wyoming to ride McCall. He asked me to meet him for a day on the snow. I agreed and a small group joined. As an instinct, I checked the weather as always when planning a ride and it called for several inches of new snow during the day and night before with partly sunny skies for our ride. Perfect!

I woke up that morning with pretty significant spasms in my leg and I almost backed out of the ride, but I decided it would most likely taper off as I got my day underway. I didn't get to see Jon very often so I was very motivated to go ride with him. It was again a weird feeling to load up and road trip down to McCall. Part of the group we were meeting at the trailhead had been with me on the road trip the morning of the avalanche. Today, we were leaving from the New Meadows lot, the same lot we had left from on March 1, 2009. This was my first time back to this lot since leaving it that March morning and sending the group back for their somber ride home—short one rider. I took a different ride out 22 months earlier—or I should say, flight.

This time on the road trip down, my phone had signaled when it received a new e-mail from the Payette Avalanche Center. I had recently signed on to receive an e-mail every time there was an updated avalanche advisory. Two years prior, I had checked it on the web periodically but now I wanted to be the guy that knew every time there was a change in conditions. I even post on Facebook and send texts to friends when the avy danger is significant.

> *I just have to keep on keepin' on. God put my eyes in the front of my head for a reason: to look forward, not back.*

I knew I had lost more motor function and strength in my only hand when we unloaded at the lot. Two weeks prior, I had been able to start my sled but today, I didn't stand a chance at hanging on to the handle under the compression. And I immediately knew that I would have a hard time operating throttle and brake and hanging on with my hand the way that it was. I gave it a shot anyway. A few miles up the trail, I was struggling and advised the group to go on, that I would head back to the truck and wait for their return. I wasn't going to wreck anyone's day, as it had turned out to be mostly sunny and beautiful with a fresh blanket of snow.

So, now as I write, I'm sitting in the truck in the parking lot staring at the trail I rode off on two years ago. I'm here again, but a new man. As a new author, I'm learning that I never leave town without my computer pack, for days like today. I'm geared up to write for you. I just stepped out of the truck for a stretch to the sound of a helicopter passing by overhead. As you can imagine, my first thought was, "I hope someone in the group didn't go for a ride." Then, I saw that it wasn't headed the right direction to be flying to the hospital. I stopped and reflected on what it must have been like to be my friends that March afternoon 22 months prior. Hearing the sounds of the blades chopping the air as it lifted off with their unconscious friend aboard must have been very difficult, to say the least. It gave me chills to think about it.

In the few weeks following, I continued to lose ground on my recovery. The regression affected my balance, coordination, and left leg motor. The biggest concern was that the weakness in my right hand continued to plague me and even increase. It was extremely frustrating and at times the loss of motor and strength in my only hand took me to tears.

I had learned to live pretty well with one hand, but it was becoming very challenging to function with not one hand, but half of a hand. I continued to fight to button my pants, put on socks and shoes, turn knobs, and even buckle Caleb's car seat. I had gone forward at a respectable rate up to this point and it became very challenging to keep my head in the game while going backwards.

I met with my doctor and requested that we hold off on the EMG and instead do a spinal MRI to see if something had changed. I feared that I may have re-injured the spine with my increased level of activity. As I lay all scrunched up in the tube, I started thinking about the number of times I had been in for scans. I realized that between MRI's and CT scans, it was my tenth time in the tube.

The MRI results showed nothing to be concerned about so we scheduled the EMG nerve test for my right arm to attempt to narrow it down to the root of the problem. In a therapy evaluation, we discovered that my left leg strength and coordination had fallen back to where it was when I had first been able to stop using the cane.

As difficult as it was, I knew that our only choice was to go back to that point and duplicate the therapy routine we had done to get me walking strong. I was well aware that doing nothing would produce just that: nothing. I continued to work out at the gym on my own a couple of days a week and we added to that a couple of days of physical therapy.

I remember telling myself again, "Matt, focus the things you can change." Those who were around during my recovery have also heard me say something over and over. I said it again with this setback: "I just have to keep on keepin' on." God put my eyes in the front of my head for a reason, *to look forward, not back.*

Potratz Boys, Back Together in Wyoming

Keepin' On

Late in the winter, we scheduled a very special ride in Wyoming. My dad was coming from Seattle, Chris from Reno, and myself from Lewiston, to stay with Jon in Wyoming and the three Potratz boys and dad were getting back on the snow together. Because we're all so spread out, this doesn't happen as much as it once did, but it was finally set up again for the first time in about three winters.

I would have only been able to hang on and operate my controls safely for a short distance so we improvised: I sat in front of Jon, stayed low and hung on to the middle of the handlebars, while he rode standing up, and we moved in sync with each other. Tim and I had done this for a full day a few years prior in Canada when my sled struck a rock and damaged the drive system. However, I had two hands then.

Jon and I were still able to jump off the trail and weave through the trees a little and even climb a few small hills. The four Potratz guys weren't shrunk to three—we got back on the snow together once again!

As I write today, it's summer again. I may be a sledhead and love snow, but 90 degrees and sunshine makes my body function and feel much better! I'm still fighting slow regression even as I type these words. I recently had four additional MRI scans on my cervical, thoracic, and lumbar spine as well as on my brain, looking to narrow down the problem. We believe that it is potentially additional cell death along the spinal cord.

When I originally injured my spine, the vertebrae didn't puncture the spinal cord. If they had, I would be a quadriplegic as some of my new friends are—and maybe you are too. If so, I have *tremendous* respect for what you do every day. As you remember from the Mayo Clinic, the vertebrae were literally only millimeters from doing so. However the injury did cause significant cell damage along the cord leading to potential paralysis, therefore the reason for the wheel chair to the cane to walking to still the inability to run.

Although a vast majority of our human cells can regenerate, neuro cells do not. Over that time period, the damaged area healed to a certain degree and the remaining neuro cells helped to compensate for the loss. We now believe that additional cells were damaged in the original injury, but hung on. However, their life span was reduced from the damage and they are possibly dying off at this point. We haven't confirmed this particular diagnosis and I'm in the process of sending records to the University of Washington neurologists in hopes for treatment options. Only time will tell.

You Can't Hit Rewind

I'm often asked if I regret riding like I rode—if I regret the risk. My answer is quickly, "No, not a bit." I've even been asked, "How can you go out and ride like that when you have a responsibility as a father to three boys?"

Yes, I am aware that my boys need me in their lives, tremendously. What I did on a snowmobile may have appeared to be "crazy," but I view it differently. Yes, many of the climbs and maneuvers were intense. Yes, they gave me a huge rush. But, as far as risk and danger, I calculated it before every move I made.

In twelve years, I racked up nearly 20,000 miles of backcountry seat time. I was a true professional. I wasn't "out of control" or "riding over my head" as some riders may be. I knew my sled very well and rode on the edge of, but within my ability. Before I climbed a technical chute, I analyzed it entirely to map my route and a possible escape route if something went wrong.

Sometimes there was no escape route. Once committed, there was only one option; over the top. When analyzing, I didn't envision myself making it

half way, I envisioned my skis cresting over the top. When it was time to go, my eyes were on the top, and unless an obstacle took my eyes away for a few seconds, they never left the top of the mountain.

Whether you think you can make it, or think you won't, you are usually right. I had done it enough times to make a good judgment call and most times I crested the top following a beautiful, trouble free ascent.

According to the U.S. Census Bureau, in 2008, the year before my avalanche, there were 10.2 million car accidents in the U.S. resulting in 39,000 fatalities. In the 2008-2009 winter, the winter that my avalanche occurred, there were 27 avalanche related deaths in the U.S., 16 were snowmobilers (The Free Resource). No, I didn't forget to put a thousand behind those numbers.

I'm aware that there is a significant amount more people that drive vehicles than ride snowmobiles, but if you were thinking, "How could he take that risk?" I genuinely and humbly ask you to reconsider. Although very risky, I don't recommend walking or riding a bicycle to work because of the danger in driving your car.

I write all of this simply to lay the foundation for this: don't live in a box for fear of something bad happening. We live in a dangerous world but I encourage you to get out and live! You only get one chance. You can't hit rewind and try again. God has provided us with a ton of incredible activities to partake in while on this earth. I agree with David Foster when he wrote:

> *"You won't find your dreams in your e-mail folder or your mailbox. Get up, get out, meet life halfway, and see what you discover."*

I ask that you join us—and live until you die.

- 8 -

NO RISK, NO REWARD

"It is not because things are difficult that we do not dare. It is because we do not dare that things are difficult."

Seneca

As I've said many times, hope was a vital part of my recovery, and it still is today. As I was continuing to fight for hope, I was having a hard time mentally overcoming the non-stop intense nerve pain. I've talked to a handful of people with the same injury and they agree; words cannot describe. We can't explain it well enough for you to understand the physical and mental challenge behind this type of pain.

Here's the kicker; if we cut our arm off, the pain remains! It's phantom! In a discussion with my pain doctor, I practically insisted that we had to do something. I couldn't stand to envision my future with constant daily pain of this magnitude. He agreed that we needed to investigate a long term remedy outside of heavy doses of pain medication.

We first looked at the possibility of a spinal cord stimulator. The stimulator would put an electrode in place in the spine at the place of injury. The electrode would carry a signal that would ultimately trick the signal to the brain to not feel the pain. We would first do a trial where x-ray was used to install the electrodes with wires coming out of the skin. If effective in the four or five day trial, the wires and control unit would all be surgically installed under the skin. I would then pack a remote to turn the unit on and off and adjust the intensity. Once or twice a week, I would charge the control unit through my skin by placing the charger on my skin over the unit. It sounded like a lot to mess with but if it worked, it would be so worth it.

The initial install was disappointing. By X-ray vision, my doctor pushed the electrodes in as far as he could and powered them up. I felt nothing at first but as the intensity increased, I began to feel the pain dissipate. It was awesome! But my abdominal area also lit up with electrical pulse, a very intense, uncomfortable pulse. He turned it off and pulled everything back out. We met in the room next door to discuss results.

My heart was pounding, looking for hope; but the pounding would soon stop as he explained, "Matt, I know you don't want to know this, but it won't work. I had the intensity on the highest setting to accomplish any pain relief at all. The problem with that is that you would feel that intense pulse in your abdomen all day. And, the system is not designed to operate on max power all the time."

The reason we had been unable to see more results from the signal was the placement of the electrodes. He explained to me that the vertebrae had been crushed down far enough to block the path in which they needed to place the electrode. He went on to say, "I know it's disappointing, but after seeing what

I saw today, you have reason to be thankful. You can walk, and that almost got taken away from you."

He closed with, "I'm researching one more idea that may work for you." I drove away nearly in tears but went back to work to get my mind on something at the dealership, and not on disappointment and pain.

Hope On The Radar

The following week I met with my pain doctor again to discuss one last option. At a conference, he had come into contact with a doctor from Chicago who specialized in specific procedures to tackle phantom nerve pain. There was a chance to possibly use a similar stimulator system at the brain. The electrodes would be placed at the brain level to interrupt the signal there instead. He was confident there were also options in addition to this and suggested that I at least go meet with this doctor to explore the options. An official referral was booked and my records were sent to Chicago. I flew to Chicago with hope on the radar! Becoming pain free would literally change my life at this point!

Chicago was so big, and even a little intimidating. I had been there once before but hadn't spent time in the heart of downtown. Northwestern Memorial Hospital is located right in the middle of it all. This small town boy from Idaho wasn't used to fifty story buildings. This trip, I had come alone. My brain was processing well enough to travel with just minor handicap assistance to substitute for long walks in the airport.

I fought at times to process multiple tasks at once, but I've been told many times "That's because you're a man." So maybe it was normal, but not the normal Matt I had known before. Although all the women who know me would disagree, I had been decent at multi-tasking. Now, it was overwhelming to process it all at the same time.

Once you settle into downtown Chicago, it's quite beautiful and majestic. I made the walk down the block to the hospital to familiarize myself for the next morning. Over dinner, I again reflected back on my journey. My left arm was hanging motionless and the pain was intense, but I had so much to be thankful for. God had given me back my brain to an extent that was unexpected.

I could walk fairly normal and smoothly down the streets of Chicago. My boys got their daddy back! I was learning to love life from a whole new angle and God was molding me into a better man every day. But, my thoughts were fogged by medication and my body still plagued with pain. I had to find a remedy. That was my mission in Chicago.

The next morning, I met the neurosurgeon I had been referred to and discussed my options. He had already looked over my records, and after an evaluation, he presented the two surgical procedures I could choose from.

He didn't think it would be necessary to go to my brain. The first possibility was to install a spinal cord stimulator from a different angle hoping to access the specific location of the nerve injury. It would require the same wiring and hardware as the stimulator in my trial back in Lewiston.

The second option was a little scary, but from my point of view, had a major advantage. They would access the base of the nerves that were sending the false signal and with a hot needle, put lesions across two nerve roots at the entry zone. The procedure was called a Dorsal Root Entry Zone Lesion, known as a DREZ Lesion.

The big advantage was that there would be no probe, wires, or any other hardware like the stimulator required. If it worked, they would sew me back up and send me home, pain free. I would lose the sensation I had regained and never have sensation in that hand again. But, no sensation means no pain.

He also explained that my case was somewhat rare in the sense that some of the nerve fibers that had been re-routed at the Mayo clinic were sensory fibers and had been routed to give my hand some sensitivity if successful. So, he explained that unlike most cases, I had a chance to eventually have a little sensation.

There was, however a disadvantage: risk. In order to access the nerve root zone, he would have to essentially go inside the spinal cord, exposing spinal fluid and all. He would complete the fragile surgery and then seal me back up. He explained that although rare, there was a chance for some spinal fluid leakage post-surgery which would result in headaches and lack of balance. There was also a low percentage chance of a slight change in left leg motor from general trauma as the left leg nerves were in close proximity to the nerves being cut.

This was a lot to consider, so he said he understood if I wanted some time to decide, even overnight if needed. I, however, felt an immediate peace about it. I asked a few more questions about the procedure. I found it to be somewhat difficult to be responsible for a decision involving such a vital part of my body. But, after careful evaluation, I spoke up and told him that I wanted to move forward with the DREZ Lesion. He was a bit surprised that I had decided so quickly and said, "Wow, that was quick. Well, it's your body and only you know what you want. Are you sure? Once we're in there, there's no turning back."

"Doc," I said, "I know there's risk to think about but I've taken a lot of risk in life and it's usually paid off. No risk, no reward. Let's get it set up."

We discussed more details and on my way out, with a handshake, my surgeon said, "Matt, I know it's a little scary. But, my hands will be the only hands inside of your body. I've done this procedure many times and I feel that I'm good at it."

I didn't take that comment as arrogant. Instead, I was encouraged by his confidence. He wasn't aware that actually, there would be two sets of hands involved, because God's hands are always in the restoration business.

No Turning Back

We scheduled the surgery for the following Monday. I calculated the cost of meals and accommodations to stay in Chicago until surgery day and found it to be nearly equivalent to flying back home. So, back in the sky I would go the next morning to intensify the nerve pain with altitude one last time.

That night Downtown Chicago was alive! The Blackhawks were competing for the Stanley Cup. My TGI Fridays® dinner was full of energy as every television in the building was tuned in to the game and cheers ignited as their team battled on the ice. Back in my room, I was notified of the Blackhawks' victory when the city erupted!

Looking down from my room, I saw every lane full; bumper to bumper, they honked and cheered, with many walking on the sidewalks cheering also. Being a small town Idaho boy, I had never seen such a thing. It went on into the early hours of the morning. Though it cost me some sleep, I considered it an honor that I got to experience the energy of their victory.

I arrived back in Chicago Sunday night and the feeling was honestly electric in the sense that fear was fighting excitement. I thought; if it works, I'll relax for the first time in 15 months! Finally, it was my hope to eliminate the constant pain I had battled for almost 11,000 hours—that's 660,000 minutes!

June 14th, 2010 is a day I'll never forget. The doctor opened me up and went to work on his 5 hour operation to potentially change my life. A mishap could change my life, but a successful procedure would give me my life back.

I woke from the surgery with a feeling I had not felt since March 1st of the previous year! I had pain from the incision and procedure but no nerve pain in my hand, just tingling! My doc did range of motion routines with each limb, to find that everything still worked! I had a few days of recovery ahead but I was on cloud nine! As soon as they let me use my phone, I called family and friends with the amazing news! Finally!

The first time out of bed was a little discouraging. I struggled to walk and had to face using another cane for a while. They ensured me that I would recover quickly as my body was merely traumatized from the invasive surgery.

After a few days of recovery, I feared trying to get back through the airport alone. As always, I was hesitant to ask for help; but I didn't have to. My sister called to tell me she was putting work and life on hold, and flying out to get her brother back home.

You Are More

Before the surgery, I had started to make myself available to speak to different groups with my powerful story and the life message it carries. That night in our hotel, Jessica told me about a song she had recently listened to that jumped out at her. She said in a convincing voice, "It's a song you've got to use in a slide show or something for your presentations." We tuned it on via internet and listened to *You Are More*, the Tenth Avenue North song she was referring to. I agreed it was powerful and planned to use it at my next opportunity. We battled our way through the busy airport and got on a flight back to the majestic Northwest.

I had been advised to take some downtime to heal but honestly, if it wasn't for spellcheck, I couldn't even *spell* downtime. I went back to work two days later in a neck brace, back on a cane, and a few more meds added to my mix. I was also scheduled to speak at a high school basketball camp that first week home. I contacted Tom at 509 Films to help me with a slide show to use at the camp to the song my sister had introduced me to. We were pressed on time, but he put a beautiful piece together.

I met him on my way to the event to pick up the finished copy. I was going to be playing a slideshow I had yet to see. But my confidence in Tom's work left me without a worry. I had also arranged for something special for myself and the young athletes: a significant influence in my life, my own high school basketball coach and teacher joined me to introduce me before I shared. You had the privilege of hearing from him in the Foreword of this book.

I kicked it off with a highlight video of me riding, followed by the actual avalanche footage. As I walked out and began to share my story, I was amazed at how tuned in and attentive the audience of young people were. I started to think, "Maybe *this* is what I want to do for a living." The time came for the new slide show and as it started, I fought back the tears as some amazing still shots that Tom had captured of me riding in various film shoots filled the screen one by one. Those shots were followed by powerful photos of my storm from coma to therapy to back on my feet. The song finished with the photos taken of me back on the seat just a few months prior.

I looked out across a crowd of young people who had been impacted by the photos, but the words of the song had touched them even deeper. These words wrenched tears from their eyes that night:

There's a girl in the corner
With tear stains on her eyes
From the places she's wandered
And the shame she can't hide

She says, "How did I get here?
I'm not who I once was.
And I'm crippled by the fear
That I've fallen too far to love

But don't you know who you are,
What's been done for you?
Yeah don't you know who you are?

You are more than the choices
    that you've made,
You are more than the sum of
    your past mistakes,
You are more than the problems
    you create,
You've been remade.

Well she tries to believe it
That she's been given new life
But she can't shake the feeling
That it's not true tonight
She knows all the answers

And she's rehearsed all the lines
And so she'll try to do better
But then she's too weak to try
But don't you know who you are?

'Cause this is not about what
    you've done,
But what's been done for you.
This is not about where you've been,
But where your brokenness brings
    you to

This is not about what you feel,
But what He felt to forgive you,
And what He felt to make you loved.

You are more than the choices
    that you've made,
You are more than the sum of
    your past mistakes,
You are more than the problems
    you create,
You've been remade.

from YOU ARE MORE, *by Tenth Avenue North*

As the song faded, repeating, *"You've been remade,"* they saw a picture of me staring at the mountain in the background, the mountain that had crushed me just 12 months and 6 days before the photo was taken.

I followed the song up with a message on "identity." I encouraged them, "You are more than the 'stuff' in life. You run so much deeper. " I urged them not to wrap their identity up in sports, parties, clubs, church, school, or whatever it may be. Instead, to know who they are as a person, and believe in that person.

My coach and I had dinner afterwards and we discussed the outcome of the presentation. He eventually spoke up to say, "Matt, I've been in this for a long time and as a teacher, coach, and now a principle, I've been around a ton of kids. Rarely, if ever have I seen a group of young people that attentive to a speaker. They were glued on you and not a sound came out of that crowd. With this story and message, I think you have something here."

Finally, the Reward

The recovery from Chicago required the quantity of different medications to climb to seven. But I knew it was temporary and that in time, I could be med-free! I had traded nerve pain for neck pain but a completely different kind of pain; with the right pillow and position, this pain would dissipate. There was no angle or position that had ever affected my phantom pain. I wasn't bothered by the neck pain because it too, was temporary.

After some time passed and my incision began to heal, I started to plan for medication elimination. I was back down to my two primary meds: Lyrica® and Hydrocodone, both of which I had been on for 15 months. After my experience with quitting Oxycontin® cold turkey, I didn't fear the process; especially because this time, I would taper them. I fought through many days of sickness and discomfort over the month that it took to taper off each of the two, one at a time. My body had become accustomed to consistently being fed those same chemicals each and every day, two or three times a day. Again, I took them away, and my body was telling me about it.

As time wore on, my days started feeling brighter and my eyes got their sparkle back. I was *finally* drug free, with the exception of occasional over the counter pain meds for the neck and general pain. For over 450 days, I popped those pills in my mouth just to keep the pain bearable and get through the day. Now, only tablets of vitamins and health & wellness supplements would be popped in and swallowed. *Victory!*

– 9 –

ADVERSITY IS NOT AN OPTION

"There is no fear in a loud noise, only in the anticipation of it."

Alfred Hitchcock

ADVERSITY IS NOT AN OPTIONAL ITEM ON LIFE'S MENU. We live in a fast and dangerous world. At some point, life's not going to go as planned. You will face adversity. A proper response to adversity, on the other hand, is optional.

I don't share my response to adversity to say, "Woe is me." Instead, maybe you'll say, "Oh, that's me. I can apply that in my life to either avoid crisis, or condition myself for a proper response." We don't know on what scale, what the event might be, or when it will happen, but we can pretty much guarantee that at some point the wind will blow, the rain will fall. It might be in an instant, it might develop over time, but at some point, adversity WILL happen.

Don't seek adversity—but don't fear it either. Think of the most amazing person that you admire in history; more than likely, you'll find that adversity happened before the amazing unfolded. Embrace your challenges! The way that you choose to respond to what happens on any scale will truly define who you are or who you'll become in life.

As I begin to reflect back on this life-changing experience, I write these words today from where it all began. I'm back in Pierce, Idaho at "The Outback," the clean, cozy, mini-resort that my parents founded when I was in high school. I haven't spent a lot of time here since because they sold it a few years after I left home. The memories flooded back last night as I began to replay in my mind the first few times my dad let me ride one of the snowmobiles from his rental fleet. It's amazing to think back on how powerful I thought that liquid cooled 600cc machine was! I never dreamed I would someday ride not only a liquid cooled, but turbo-charged 1000cc sled with sponsor logos down the side.

I walked out this morning and looked over where the rental fleet used to line up. In that spot now sits the log cabin suite that my dad, brothers, and I built. With TWO HANDS, we had stacked each log and drove each lag. With TWO HANDS, we filled each crack, painted the trim, and put the finishing touches on a beautiful cabin. How many things do we all do in life every day that require TWO HANDS? I had done them all without thinking twice, assuming that I would always have TWO HANDS. Go with me to an average day in our lives. We use TWO HANDS all day long without thinking twice.

Now, take one away. Open a jar; it just spins on the counter. Peel a banana; you can't hold it and peel. Open a ziplock bag; you can't hold the bag in place and unzip at the same time. Open a bottle of water; the bottle turns instead of the cap. Cut a steak; there's nothing to hold it in place. Turn the pages in this book with nothing to hold it in place. Type every word you're reading with just one hand. It can be done. I'm not whining or complaining; I use my knees to hold jars and bottles. I use my teeth to twist off caps, peel back wrappers, open envelopes, hold the laundry in place to fold it, and much more. I use my feet to pry things open, hold a door in place, scoot myself into bed, push off of things, and much more.

It's amazing what you find that you can do without TWO HANDS, when life gives you no choice but to learn. Next time you struggle to find something to be thankful for in life, be thankful that you have TWO HANDS. I'm sure my friends out there living with just one hand would agree, the little stuff in life matters more, and we see life through a whole new lens.

I don't suggest that you worry and plan for the worst. But think about how you'll respond if the worst happens. Don't just think about losing a hand.

> *My weak hand typed these words, but my strong heart wrote this book.*

I encourage you to have the confidence to know how you would respond in the midst of any significant adversity. I didn't plan on struggling to walk, fighting my mind, or losing the use of an arm.

I didn't dream of one day writing a book with one hand. I didn't plan to write a book at all! Becoming a motivational speaker and life coach was not in my career plan. All of these things are shaping my new life—and because of my proper response, I'm living a more fulfilled life today than I even knew existed before. There's a lot that I can't do, but I've discovered that in my physical condition, writing, speaking, encouraging, investing in lives—all of these are things that I can do.

Henry Ford once said: *"One of the great discoveries a man makes, one of his great surprises, is to find out that he can do what he was afraid he couldn't do."* I've always enjoyed writing. My greatest surprise has been watching my life become a story worth writing about; a story that brings a new perspective on our TWO HANDS. I started writing this book in an application on my smartphone lying in bed each night. Then I bought a laptop and kept typing. It was somewhat overwhelming initially, but God told me to write this book.

Before the avalanche, I could type somewhere in the neighborhood of fifty words per minute. Every word you read was keyed in with my one hand, and it wasn't keyed at anywhere near fifty words per minute. I'm not complaining, I just slowly dance around the keyboard and never forget that my hands only do half of the work. My weak hand typed these words, but my strong heart wrote this book.

We use our hands to touch, to reach out, to grab, to hold, to hug, to shake, to direct, to paint, to design, to create, to express emotion. What if your hands can't—can your heart?

Ruled By Success

When I came home from 88 days in the hospital, I thought for sure I could condition myself back to continuing to carry out my career. My fight to be back in the workforce was grueling. Although I was relatively productive, it was obvious that it was taking every last bit of energy that I had to balance a job, my boys, therapy, and healing. Although confused and angry at first, I'm now thankful that Ryan recognized that it was going to make it challenging to be productive in recovery with the stress and long hours that my job required.

I had requested a meeting to cast some vision for training. Vision wasn't discussed for training but rather for a complete change in my future. He asked me how I felt about how the job was going. I expressed some concerns but continued to lie to myself and to him that I could do it and that I felt great.

His words were tough to hear. "Potratz, I'm not gonna lie to you, I have very high expectations of you because of who you were before. But, I don't think the new Matt can live up to those expectations. Do you? The new training position isn't working out as I'd hoped anyway."

"Not yet," I replied, "but I will be that Matt again in time." My position was cut and I was encouraged to take some time to recover and consider taking a different position in the dealership if something came available in the future.

I have always been hard on myself, at times even very critical. As a manager and leader, I held myself to a higher standard than I held anyone else to. I believe that I was even addicted to success. "Addicted to success?" you may ask. Yes. The way you determine if you're addicted to anything is to ask yourself this; does it rule my life? In my case, my drive to succeed ruled my time, talent, and resources, my life.

No matter what I was involved in, I wanted to be successful at it or I didn't want to participate. Yes, that's a good thought in moderation. However, my passion to be successful consumed me. On a snowmobile, I was talented, but I wanted to be exceptional, and I laid a lot down to get there; including time with my family. At work, I was good, but I wanted to be great, and I exhausted myself to be promoted to the top. One of my biggest fears was that of setting the bar too low and reaching or exceeding the goal. So at times, I was guilty of having unrealistic expectations of "Matt."

Up until this life-altering accident, I was very black and white when measuring my success, or as I put it, "my contribution to society." It was as simple as, am I an asset to the world I live in or am I a liability? Do I give more than I take? There was no grey area. I figured that if I wasn't an asset, then I must be a liability. So, I can remember laying in pain one day thinking, "Matt, you've become a liability; you need other people too much. You rely on healthcare, your insurance company, disability income—you take, take, take."

It was at that point I had decided that I was going to find a way to get back into the workforce, to get back to being productive sooner than doctors had suggested that I do. I had a paralyzed left arm, I couldn't walk without a cane, had residual effects from my brain injury, and I suffered from constant, debilitating, phantom nerve pain 24 hours a day, 7 days a week, all 52 weeks of the year. Yet, shortly afterward, I had made the agreement with Ryan to come back to work part time for no salary; just work as therapy. I was convinced that I could condition myself to get back on my feet and go again.

> *I began to discover a God who loved and accepted me exactly the way I was, even busted up.*

After the long and grueling process of discovering that my body was not ready to live up to what my job required, I was very critical and upset with myself. I began to cut the new Matt down and to tell myself I couldn't live up to my standards. I think I was hoping that it might motivate me to dig deep and fight harder but in all reality, only became more discouraging. I was not only unable to live up to my standards, but also unable to meet the standards set by the lifestyle I had lived before. The world as I knew it had rejected the *new me* and for the first time in my adult life, I was desperately searching for acceptance.

Then God began to speak to me in a big way. David Foster summed it up perfectly when he wrote, *"God allows us to feel rejected by others in order to seek the only acceptance that matters: His!"* I began to discover a God who loved and accepted me exactly the way that I was, even busted up. He started to chip away at my "liability" mentality when he spoke to me very clearly one day.

"Matt, in your darkest hour, in your state of coma with a breathing tube and feeding tube in place, your body plagued with paralysis, I still valued you more than I valued my own Son. He values you enough that even on your death bed at your lowest low, He would have allowed them to drive those spikes through his hands and hang him on the cross to die that painful death even if you were the only one he was dying for—because you are worth it."

Wow! I don't have to tell you that was a life changing message from God! If the banged up "Matt" was worth a sacrifice of that magnitude, it's obvious that the word "liability" is not a part of God's vocabulary.

My black and white mentality has, and is, changing—and I understand now that in some seasons of life, we may need life to give back to us. I now view success in life as simple as this: in the big picture, do I live a life more fulfilled by "giving" than by "getting?"

It's okay to set the bar high. Just keep it realistic and allow yourself to feel a sense of accomplishment from time to time. You cannot give more than you have. God created you to believe in yourself and be confident in the man or woman he created you to be.

> *You've got to be humble and disciplined enough to be your biggest critic, yet confident enough to be your biggest fan.*

You've got to be humble and disciplined enough to be your biggest critic, yet confident enough to be your biggest fan. Know when you've missed the mark and where you need to focus your efforts in order to get better, but reach your capability by trusting your God given ability to see it through.

Adversity is a Gift

Adversity often uncovers new ways to give. You might end up giving gifts that you never knew existed, gifts that were never possible before the road got rough. I could have easily spoken to groups before my avalanche. I had the ability, but I had nothing captivating to speak about. *Adversity delivered it.* I could have reached out to encourage a family with a loved one in the hospital, but I'm just an outsider with no true understanding. I walked through the valley of the shadow of death and now they seek me out to walk through it with them. *Adversity delivered it.* I had the ability to write well as a businessman, but I had

no reason to write a book. *Adversity delivered it.* Unwrap the gifts that adversity delivers! Don't seek out adversity. Seek out the opportunity to give in the midst of adversity and it will astonish you what you can accomplish when your ruins are transformed to beauty.

Adversity gave me the opportunity to give back an incredible gift to the very people who saved my life at ground zero. While speaking at the St. Alphonsus Medical Center Ski and Mountain Trauma Conference in Sun Valley, Idaho, I had the opportunity to re-connect with the EMS crew that transported me by sled from the mountain to the helicopter. There were hugs and handshakes that will never be forgotten.

We connected later to organize a small session with McCall Fire and Rescue and their families back in McCall. I went down to an evening business meeting and dinner with fire and rescue staff and their families. They got to hear why they do what they do. They told me that after they close the doors on the Ambulance at the hospital or the chopper door before liftoff, they rarely, if ever, see the happy endings.

I ended my presentation with passion as I spoke, "Guys, this is an incredible medical and survival story but if we push all that aside and go back to day one, in the rubble of an avalanche; if you had not applied your training and done your job well, none of the rest would matter. My story would have ended that day. You gave three boys their daddy back. What you do doesn't go un-noticed, it matters more than words can tell. Thank you for what you do." I looked out across a room of teary eyes, smiling faces, and warmed hearts. *Adversity delivered it.*

The night continued to make memories. They took me out to see the rescue sled that transported me. I was again overwhelmed with appreciation for what they did to get me out of that rugged backcountry. It was their turn to bring tears to my eyes. They handed me a marker and said, "Will you do us the honor of signing your name on the shell of this sled?"

My eyes got a little wet, followed by a big smile as I made the last stroke of the marker. *Matt Potratz* left a piece of his heart imprinted on that rescue sled. The moment was not a gift to them, but to me; a gift inspired by adversity. Adversity delivered encouragement and motivation to my new friends that risk their lives daily for those that they don't even know.

I was given yet another opportunity to give. I was speaking at a church in Boise and I knew exactly how I would spend my afternoon downtime; I went back to the hospital. First, all the memories of wheelchair rides outside flooded back as I walked along the pathways. When I stepped out of the elevator and into the Intensive Care Unit, I felt amazing, and once again felt that same strong sense of appreciation.

One of the nurses walking by stopped and said, "Hey, wait a minute. Are you that snowmobile guy!? The one that was caught in an avalanche?"

"Yep, that's me," I responded with a smile.

She was amazed and said, "Oh my gosh, you look amazing!" She finished what she was doing and led me to the nurses' station to see more of my heroes. I didn't re-unite with all of my doctors and nurses that day, but the ones that were there genuinely thanked me for inspiring them with my visit.

I then said, "One more thing, I'll be right back." I went down the elevator and back to my truck. I prepared a simple gift and marched it back inside. I told the girls at the counter, "This is the first hat that my clothing sponsor HMK ever gave me. It's got some hours on it and some hair fell out in it, so I'm leaving some Matt Potratz behind for ya. I also signed the bill for you. Put this on the shelf over there and every time you see it, you'll remember that what you do really matters." Once again, there were shiny eyes. *Adversity delivered that gift.* They will all agree that when properly responded to, adversity is a gift. I'm confident that as you read this book, it keeps on giving.

Stop and Have a Glass of Lemonade

One day late in my recovery, God gave me an awesome vision as I was praying. In the vision I was mowing the lawn one hot afternoon. I looked over and saw Jesus in a chair in the shade off to the side drinking lemonade with ice cubes. I was half way done and shut the mower off to empty the grass bag. Jesus said "Hey Matt, come over and have a glass of lemonade."

I had a very dry mouth, so I thought about it but then replied, "I can't right now, the lawn is only half done, I've got to finish first and then maybe I will."

He said, "It's hot out here, you must be thirsty. Come and be refreshed. There'll be plenty of time to finish." I walked over, took the extra glass of ice cold lemonade he was holding out, and sat down in the chair beside him.

> *Don't try to **take** the time, because I promise you that many times it won't be there. Instead, **make** the time.*

As a borderline perfectionist, I always have to have the mower tire tracks perfectly lined up so when looking at the lawn, the lines are perfectly straight. I had a couple friends ask me, "Is that really necessary?" When I was married, even my boys' mom said, "What difference does it make? It's just grass!" To me it was necessary and it did matter, but I began to think, "Maybe I am being ridiculous. Maybe it is stupid." Regardless, I continued to mow that way and still do today.

But in the vision, while enjoying our lemonade, Jesus said something cool. He was looking at the half of the lawn I had finished, chuckled and said, "Look at those lines, perfectly straight—as always. Now that your thirst is quenched, I'm sure you'll make the second half look just as good. Matt, its okay to want the lines so straight, just be sure you stop to have a glass of lemonade."

This vision spoke volumes to me! How many times in life had I, and perhaps you, get so caught up in the busyness of life and making sure everything is in order, that we don't leave time to stop and have a glass of lemonade?

Don't think of just lemonade. *I don't even like lemonade!* The glass of lemonade might be the kids' ball game you missed, a friend that was in need, your spouse needed love and encouragement, a fun day with your family, a fishing trip, and the list could go on.

Or maybe, your spiritual thirst needs quenched. You need to spend some time on your knees, or sit down and knock the dust off the book of lemonade—or book of life, whichever you prefer to call it—and dig in for a thirst quenching. As you read this now, examine your life. What areas can you *make* the time to stop and have a glass of lemonade? Don't try to *take* the time, because I promise you that many times it won't be there. Instead, *make* the time. If you choose to make the time, the result is guaranteed.

A proper response to adversity requires the willingness to stop and have a glass of lemonade. Is your dry mouth causing the mower to veer off track in your family, at work, or in your life in general? What happens when the glass shatters and all of the lemonade that you haven't been drinking splashes on the floor? Have you ever tried to gather that back up to drink it again? Not going to happen! Life truly is short. Take it from me, it can change or even end quite quickly. Quench your thirst. Take it all in. Suck on the ice cubes if you have to. Don't miss a drop of the lemonade in your life.

Embrace It

Adversity will happen on some scale, at some time. I promise you, you can't change that. However, don't live in fear of it. It's not as scary as you think—if you make the proper choices in the midst of it. Regardless of the severity, don't look at the damage your adversity has done or could do. Instead, find out what can be done, and how it can change you. Be willing to accept that it's not an option. Don't run from adversity. When you face it, *embrace it.*

212 DEGREES

"*A pessimist is one who makes difficulties of his opportunities, and an optimist is one who makes opportunities of his difficulties.*"

Harry Truman

IN THE SECOND CHAPTER I MENTIONED THAT 212 IS MY OLDEST BOY CONNOR'S BIRTHDAY AND WAS MY RACE NUMBER ON MY MOTORCYCLE. 212 is also a significant number in chemistry and in life. 212 degrees is the boiling point of water. We've all watched it happen as water goes from still to rumbling when it reaches that threshold. When we take a closer look, there is real significance at that moment.

That boiling point is a transformation point. The water is transformed from calm and still, to boiling, and things start to happen. If you're a parent like me, you're probably a professional "Mac and Cheese Chef." You'll agree that if you pour the noodles in before the water boils, nothing happens. Instead, if you pour them in after the bowling point, the transformation, activity starts to happen! If you don't boil the noodles long enough, they come out either crunchy or too chewy and the transformation of the noodle fails. But if everything is done right, the water is brought to a boil, the noodles are cooked exactly as directed, the milk, butter, and cheese are properly added; a transformation takes place! Little dry, crunchy noodles are changed into soft, creamy, cheesy bowls of macaroni. And the chef proudly serves it up.

> *I got wrapped up in Matt's agenda and remained a dinky little crunchy noodle.*

Apply this concept to your life. We don't want to reach our boiling point because transformation happens, good or bad. Healthy transformation means change, and being stretched outside of our crunchy comfort zone. God took me to my boiling point. I had been in the water, but I'd become comfortable as an uncooked, wet noodle. I had the type of personality and possessed character traits that if I had allowed God to transform me, I could have invested in and participated in transforming lives long before the avalanche. But I got wrapped up in Matt's agenda and remained a dinky little crunchy noodle. God allowed the heat to intensify and the water hit the bowling point. The microscope got off of Matt and gave me a wider scope to see the macaroni around me.

It's been painful but this noodle named Matt has been transformed and I'm mixing in the cheese a little every day. The boiling bounced me around the pot a little and cost me an arm, strength and energy, and some ability, but it transformed my heart into a soft, moldable noodle that God can work with. I'm also learning that I'm not the only noodle in the pot. I'm finding those who didn't boil long enough and helping them get back in life's water. Others rumbled through the transformation and just need a little help getting in the cheese sauce.

Take me to 212! When I speak and look out across an attentive crowd that's soaking in the message, I want to stay on the verge of boiling! It's not about Matt anymore, and if it becomes about me, I want to go right back to boiling. Humility has become one of my most valuable attributes and I wouldn't trade it for anything. If it's all about me, the focus is on what I don't have and need to gain. When I shift the spotlight to others, I focus on what I do have and need to give. I'm not just talking about giving material things. Sometimes we'll give those things, but most of the giving that God requests will come from the heart; time, talent, love, friendship, encouragement, etc.

Now that I'm viewing life through a new lens, it's painful at times to see the tremendous need for people to fill that gap and give those gifts. Take something as simple as *time*. What if for one day, everyone in this crazy, busy world would see a need, fill a need, and give just a little time to someone in their life? This world would transform in one day into the most perfect bowl of macaroni ever prepared! It's chef, our Creator, would serve it up with pride.

We are all in a different pot with different liquids and ingredients. We all have a different boiling point. I hope that you're boiling point doesn't require the intense heat that I rumbled through. But if it does, embrace it! Jim Rohn was right on the money when he said, *"Choice, not circumstance, determines your success."* Choose to allow your boiling to mold and change you.

Be the Change

You've heard me say, "focus on the things you can change," a handful of times in this book. It's a simple phrase, but probably the most effective concept in my successful recovery. I've recited those seven words to myself literally hundreds of times. My energy reserves were very low and I couldn't afford to waste valuable energy. I learned that if I couldn't impact or change it, I couldn't spare the energy to worry about or to even think about it. I disciplined myself to channel the energy that I did have only toward things that mattered, and that I could impact. Again, I don't stress about or curse the avalanche; it's done. I can't change it. I don't complain about my dead arm, I just do the therapy routine. I can't change whether it comes back to life or not. I don't whine out about how I struggle to walk. I just focus on a smooth motor pattern and walk on. I can't change how much I struggle each day. No need to cry about it. I just apply my energy to putting the pieces back where they fit and finding a home for the new pieces God has given me. In your life; how many times do you get hung up wasting time and energy on things you cannot change? What if every day you were to harness all of your time and energy to be focused only on things that you can impact? No more exhausting yourself in frustration over things you can't control.

When your focus is in line, you can move on to *"be the change you want to see."* Do something! Don't just talk about what you're going to change, change it! Be the change. You'll be amazed by the impact when you apply these two principles in your life. Focus on the things you can change, and be the change you want to see. It will change your world.

Battling Crisis

Depression seemed to always remain at my doorstep, just waiting for me to plunge into the negative. I had to guard my heart and mind. I chose to expose myself to Prayer Counseling through my home church to help fight it off. It was very effective as we looked to God for guidance.

In addition, the boiling has taught me that the best way to tackle the feeling of depression was to get my mind off of "me." I began to use my experience to invest in the lives of others who were fighting similar battles with depression. I found that what I've been through gives me a platform to reach them. They connect because they know that I know how they feel; that I can really understand. I've found healing for my own frustration and hurt when I help others uncover their hurt and find healing. God began to break my heart for those wading through any kind of crisis.

Soon, you'll see me fulfill my new dream to launch a crisis rehabilitation center. With God at the foundation, we'll offer professional encouragement, counseling, accountability, tests, family support, and guidance through crisis. The crisis might be an accident like I've been through, drug or alcohol addiction, disaster, or anyone in need of love and encouragement.

Many times I've thought, *what if?* What if I hadn't had the amazing network of family and friends that I have? *What if* I hadn't been surrounded with positive energy, guidance, or someone to believe in me? What if I didn't have God?

The answer is pure and simple: without those variables, I would not have come out of my crisis as physically, mentally, or emotionally whole. I'm thankful that because of that support, I have my health, and a sound mind to be thankful for that, good friends to invest my love and trust in, and God to walk with me to tomorrow's door.

I have a promising future! The "what if" thoughts ignited the fire in my heart to launch the rehab support center. We'll find those with little or no family and friends, and be the family. If they need someone to talk to, we'll be the ears. If they need a visitor in the hospital, we'll be that friend. If they're starving for positive energy, they can feed off of us. My heart is to change the world one crisis at a time.

Loving "Me"

Part of going through the transformation at my boiling point was learning to love myself. Yes, I said love *myself.* Not to be big and proud, but to value who I am. Notice I didn't say *what* I am, I said *who* I am. I've mentioned that concept a handful of times in this book. You cannot effectively love anyone until you first love *you*. You cannot value anyone until you value you. I have learned to love *who* this life changing experience has transformed me into.

He then pointed to the swings at the end that are designed for handicap kids to sit in and said, "Dad, I can't swing in those swings. Those are for people like you."

If you look up "who" in the dictionary, Webster's and nearly every other refers to the *person*. The definition of "person" refers to "a living human, an individual." The *individual* I have become is still "Matt," just a more humble, more real, more selfless version. "What" I have become is a pretty banged up, partially paralyzed, uncoordinated, slower version of Matt. "Who" I have become is beautiful, and I get to play a part in changing lives every day.

Although I don't find my identity in *what* I am, I do have to accept *what* I am. The fall following the Chicago DREZ lesion surgery, Connor was ready to start kindergarten. It was fun the first time that dad got to take him to school, but I have to admit, reality also stepped into the ring. My little boy was growing up, and I was just plain getting old! I laughed inside as I thought about it.

As we walked across the playground toward his classroom, he of course had to show me all of the cool toys. He loved to swing and said, "Daddy, these swings actually go pretty high." He then pointed to the swings at the end that are designed for handicap kids to sit in and said, "Dad, I can't swing in those swings. Those are for people like you."

I laughed and asked, "Buddy, what do you mean?"

"Well," he replied, "there's some kids in my school that must have gotten hurt like you did or something because they need those kind." I admired his perception and I was able to laugh hearing him say, "people like you" because I've learned to accept what I am and love who I am.

The Question

The question that's come up plenty during my continuing recovery battle is one I'm sure that you've also asked before: how much more of this can I handle before I break? I've even asked at times "God, where are You?" I've cried out to God, "I can't take this anymore! This is more than I can handle!" I went far enough to say, "God, please just let me go to sleep and not wake up. Take me to heaven."

I'm always encouraged that no matter what we're going through, no matter the significance, there is always truth and direction in the Bible. To answer the questions, "How much more?" and "Where are you?" here is something I ran across in the book of Jeremiah, chapter 5, verse 22:

> "I, the LORD, define the ocean's sandy shoreline as an everlasting boundary that the waters cannot cross. The waves may toss and roar, but they can never pass the boundaries I set."(NLT)

When we reach our boiling point, as the waves toss and roar, there is always hope. If He commands the massive ocean from shore to shore, he certainly commands the bounds in which the waves in life can pass.

"How much can I take?" God sets the boundaries, Hes got it under control, and no matter how bad it gets, the hope you can hang onto is that it can never pass the bounds He sets. He won't set the bounds to be more intense than we can handle. Believe it!

Your boiling point might take you past 212, but *embrace* it, knowing that you'll experience more transformation, more strength. We don't look strong because we found a way to avoid adversity. We find strength we never thought possible when we face it head on and don't fail, but *prevail.*

– 11 –
A NEW MORNING

"If we did all the things we are capable of doing,
we would literally astound ourselves."

Thomas Edison

WHEN YOU WERE BORN, YOU CRIED AND THE WORLD REJOICED. LIVE YOUR LIFE IN SUCH A MANNER THAT WHEN YOU DIE, THE WORLD CRIES AND YOU REJOICE. This Native American saying applies to any personality type, any gender, any color, any background, any living human being. Leave your mark! I'll rejoice in heaven someday looking back on the lives I touched and the positive change I inspired, the way I lived.

My world got turned upside down and transformation took place in my life. I was classified as disabled for a legitimate reason. I could have easily collected a Social Security Disability check for life. But I've never done anything centered around the word *easily*. My physical limitations are tremendous and plenty of daily pain goes with that, but I still have one good hand, a healthy mind, and a heart big enough to write a book. I kept my handicap parking permit to park close at the shopping centers—but otherwise, I'm too busy to be disabled. I chose to dig in and leave a bigger mark on this earth. Now my boys can model their lives off of what dad did in the face of adversity. Do I still cry in agony some days? You bet I do! *"The soul would have no rainbow if the eyes had no tears." (Unknown)* I dry my eyes and dig a little deeper.

While driving down the road one day listening to business training materials on CD, I had to pull over to write it down when I heard: *"Our background and circumstances may have influenced who we are, but we are responsible for who we become" (Cicero, Rome (106-43 B.C.).* I am a different man, both physically and mentally! I couldn't control the avalanche that day. I can't change how bad it crushed my body. I can do nothing to make my arm come back or bring back my gait. These factors have all influenced who I am today. However, I still have a choice; I can lay idle, or reach my new potential!

I am responsible to God to become everything the new Matt can become. He spared my life! I am responsible to love my boys and father them to the best of my ability. They need their dad! I am responsible to you, my reader, to deliver this life changing story. I take full responsibility for who I am now, and who I can still become.

What happens?

I wake up to a new morning every day. Yesterday is gone and tomorrow isn't here yet but today is in my lap. Your day is going to happen. With or without you, it will happen. You can't change that. What you can change is what happens while it happens. My day doesn't happen as smooth and simple as it used to. I have to work hard to make things happen. If I adopt the wrong attitude and outlook on my day, very little will happen. My only hand is still operating at about half of the normal strength and coordination. The finer the motor, the worse it is.

I roll out of bed to get dressed for my day and the fun begins. The neurological command to lift my left leg is not connecting from brain, to spinal cord, to leg. I grab ahold of and lift my leg up and lay it across my good leg and then slide my pant leg onto that foot. Once both legs are started, I begin to pull and my weak fingers struggle to hang on as I pull up. Now to button; laying on my back, thumb behind the button, middle finger through the button hole to pull it close, line it up, and push it through with the thumb. It's become routine, but was a fight at first without *two hands*.

> *From the moment I roll out of bed, I begin to monitor my attitude. I can promise you this: if I don't control my attitude, it controls me.*

Before the shirt, it's my newest addition to the lineup: I lay back onto my wide cloth belt, pull it into place around my abdomen, and secure the Velcro®. In a small pocket on front of the belt is a magnet. You'll soon know why.

Now for the shirt; lay it out on my lap, pick up my dead arm and push it up through the shirt to the sleeve, push my good arm and head through, and my weak hand pulls the shirt into place and straightens it up. Almost ready!

I strap on my wrist brace, also with a magnet slid down in its pocket, stand up, pick up my arm, position it where it looks somewhat natural and thud, the magnet in the wrist brace strongly connects through my shirt to the magnet in the belt, and I'm ready to go! No sling, no shoulder strap, no adjusting or resituating. I'm ready to tackle another day.

From the moment I roll out of bed, I begin to monitor my attitude. Sometimes I shed a tear or two in frustration but I don't let it wreck my day. I can promise you this: if I don't control my attitude, it controls me. If I hadn't jumped in the drivers' seat early on in my fight, I would never have climbed my massive mountain of survival and recovery. There are 24 hours in every day. I'll let you sleep a good solid 9 hours. What are you going to make happen in the remaining 900 minutes?

Plenty to Little

The title of chapter three was *Hero to Zero*. I use that term sometimes when I speak and people say, "You're not zero now, though." Very true, but I'm learning to be a humble hero now instead of the hot shot hero I was before. Was I an arrogant 'hot shot' because of all of my success? No, not really. People looked up to me and admired me because I connected with every person on any level, at any stage in life. However, I could do life without the help of anyone.

You've read about God and the Bible a handful of times in this book. I could do life without God's help too, or so I thought; He took me to *zero* in the sense that I was completely powerless, living only by the assistance of a machine. I lost nearly everything in the midst of crisis; my career, my sport, my athletic ability, my arm, my girlfriend, my dignity.

I'm not a 'Bible thumper' preacher at all, but I'm telling you friend, I only walked through the valley of the shadow of death to the place I am today because of God. My ability to keep a good attitude and stay on the right track, to inspire in the midst of significant physical and emotional pain, to rebound to *Hero,* came because I opened up the Bible for direction.

The Bible is not a book of rules and regulatrions, it's life's complete instruction manual. Think about the most complex thing you've ever assembled; did you attempt it without the instruction manual? Life is much more complex and trial and error can be painful.

> *"I know how to live on almost nothing or with everything. I have learned the secret of living in every situation, whether with a full stomach or empty, with plenty or little. For I can do everything with the help of Christ who gives me the strength I need." Philippians 4:12-13 (NLT)*

Population Me

My world has become so much more than population *me*. My days start out just me and God, as I read, meditate on, apply, and pray over what I read in my Bible. As I say Amen, God is invited to be a part of my every move throughout the day as I begin by fielding e-mails and Facebook® messages from those I befriend and encourage in their weekly walk through life.

The population of my little sphere grows throughout the day as I visit a family in the hospital, have coffee with one of my new friends fighting through drug or alcohol rehabilitation, support a young person by attending a ball game, speak to a high school student body, or lead my home-group of young men

Matt and Kayla

through our weekly Bible study. There's much more and the population in my world is difficult to even count! Your population may be much larger, it may be much smaller, but even as little as population three, is a ton more rewarding than population me.

One other very important person that populates my new world is the most recent asset that God has invested into my life: my new best friend and life partner, Kayla. For the first time in my 30 years, I didn't go out looking for love or companionship; looking to make it happen on my own. It wasn't even on the radar. God's agenda was on my radar and that has become more rewarding than any agenda I've ever composed on my own. Because I gave God the reigns; let him steer the ship, he gave me something that I had convinced myself didn't exist: someone to *share* life with.

By share, I mean just that. She shares in the victories, in the laughter, in the sorrow, in the pain, in the good days and the bad. God sent her down my path when I needed her most. My neurological setback had reached its peak and I was not just struggling physically, but mentally and emotionally as well. It was so hard to come so far, then take a giant leap backwards. I spend every day in the full-time inspiration and encouragement business with the spout of my love tank full open. I needed my love tank re-filled, I needed inspired, and God delivered, not just for a day or two but ongoing until my last day or two comes.

She also shares in my daily activities as a life coach and reaches many that I simply can't get through to. Shortly after she came into my life, God put a song on the radio that made it real to me that she was His gift. On the chorus of the song, Dave Barnes sings out:

God gave me you for the ups and downs
God gave me you for the days of doubt
For when I think I've lost my way
There are no words here left to say, it's true
God gave me you

from GOD GAVE ME YOU, *by Dave Barnes*

The following week, she brought tears to my eyes when she sent me a link to the song *"Won't Let Go"* by Rascal Flatts. This is not some soft and squishy love story, she sent it as a promise that's being put to the test even as I write today. I struggle to get up from writing to walk to the bathroom. I've had many significant falls and the arm that types these words, is scabbed up from the blood that leaks from my veins on impact.

It's real; she watches a grown man cry in frustration some days, not from the physical pain, but the agony of defeat. Together, we stand me back up to go again, to give again. Some days I give so much to those around me, that I literally have nothing left to give her. Yet, she stands by me. These words that brought tears to my eyes may soak your cheeks too:

It's like a storm
That cuts a path
It's breaks your will
It feels like that

You think your lost
But you're not lost on your own
You're not alone

I will stand by you
I will help you through
When you've done all you can do
If you can't cope
I will dry your eyes
I will fight your fight
I will hold you tight
And I wont let go

It hurts my heart
To see you cry
I know it's dark
This part of life
Oh it finds us all
And we're too small
To stop the rain
Oh but when it rains

I will stand by you
I will help you through
When you've done all you can do
And you can't cope
I will dry your eyes
I will fight your fight
I will hold you tight

And I wont, let, go.

from WON'T LET GO, *by Rascal Flatts*

As she stands by me, she's half way through the schooling required to become a nurse. I laugh when I often say, "a banged up guy like me needs my very own full-time nurse." A better bonus is that we both agree that inside a healthy sphere of influence around any of us, is never *Population Me.*

A New "Something"

Because of my reputation in the business world, when I lost my job, I had some other opportunities pop up. Employment seemed like a necessary piece of the puzzle to get back on my feet, so I wrestled with the idea—but God kept telling me no. I heard Him many times speak clearly to me, "Matt, just write the book." It was scary to think about trying to make a living as an author and speaker, especially as a rookie that no one really knew of in that world.

My dad went with me to speak at an event in Montana and on the road trip I explained to him my frustration with the situation. My argument was that, "Yes, I'm hurt, but I can still work. I want to be a productive contributor to society. I feel like I'm leaching off of the system. That's just not me." After an outstanding event, we drove home discussing our experience and I began to have the same feeling I had felt at the basketball camp after Chicago, "Maybe this *is* what I want to do."

Interacting with young fans in Lewistown, MT

I've always admired my dad for his wisdom. I want to share with you an e-mail that he sent me the following week. I still hang on to it today as a reminder that I made the right move:

"Matt,

"I've been thinking of and praying for your situation quite often and even more so since traveling with you to speak in Montana.

"You have been through more difficulties in the last 2 years than most people experience in a lifetime. Just the physical struggles alone would be more than enough to break even the strongest of people and you have had to endure many emotional struggles as well. With that said, my advice and I believe God's wisdom would be simply this; give yourself some time to heal. Your body, your mind, and your spirit all need to finish recovering!

"You have been given the opportunity to not be under tremendous pressure to have to work. Take advantage of that opportunity! Use this time to focus on your recovery, focus on your boys, focus on your speaking opportunities and finish writing your book. I believe these things need to be your priorities for the time being. I know there is tremendous pressure to "do something" that is productive in other people's eyes (i.e. work). Don't succumb to that pressure, listen for the quiet voice of the Holy Spirit and he will show you what you need to do and when you need to make a move.

"I don't believe any of the opportunities for a job will evaporate quickly because those opportunities are based on your reputation and the relationships you have built over the years. Honesty, integrity and good work ethic will reward you because you have chosen the high road as opposed to the easy way in life."

I took his advice to heart and almost immediately felt like a weight lifted. I wrote out my weekly schedule to consistently hit the gym, physical therapy, speak at a few schools and meetings, and rest.

Early in my schedule was my first big public event on December 11, 2010. The events of that evening made it a defining moment where I felt that I was leaving the business world for good, getting behind the wheel of what I do today as an author, speaker, and life coach—and driving at the speed that God tells me to. We used the large auditorium at my church, New Bridges Community Church (which I had been a part of since its birth).

I was honored to see the room fill up to standing room only and to the point that some were turned away to come back for the session the next morning.

Some people enter our lives and leave almost instantly. Others stay, can forge such an impression on our heart and soul, we are changed forever.

I had organized a live band to kick it off and give the room good energy. Highlight films were played and the room became somber as they rolled the actual video footage of the avalanche on the big screens.

As I walked out to share my heart wrenching story, I started with what had happened on the hill that day immediately following the avalanche. I had arranged to have each member of my riding crew to be there that night, but they didn't know they were coming on stage.

HMK provided me with an avalanche shovel for each member of the crew that had been there for the immediate rescue. These shovels were not something they would ever use, but something they would hang on to forever. On the blade of each shovel was professionally printed:

"To the world you may be one person, but to one person, you may be the world. Thanks for being my world on March 1ˢᵗ, 2009."

Matt with Kirk Zack, owner of HMK

I signed each shovel for them. I asked the crowd to join me in applauding my heroes. Their tears would not be the only ones shed on this special night. As I shared the story of my boys singing to me in my coma, tears broke out across the crowd. The night was only beginning. Toward the end of my speech, I began to call out the names of those who were most involved in my recovery and bring them up to join me on stage. With a nearly full stage, I thanked them with a quote followed by a roof-lifting applause:

"Some people enter our lives and leave almost instantly. Others stay, can forge such an impression on our heart and soul, we are changed forever."

I then reminded the crowd of my boys singing to me to *"Never Let Go"* and energized them when I announced that I was going to sing that song. As the band played, I started to sing the first verse: *"Even though I walk through the valley of the shadow of death, your perfect love is casting out fear..."* and the room felt amazing. But it got better. As I finished the last verse, I announced that I had three guests to join me to sing through one more time and my boys stepped out with microphones in hand and sang with me:

I can see a light that is coming for the heart that holds on
And there will be an end to these troubles
But until that day comes
Still I will praise You, still I will praise You

Oh no, You never let go
Through the calm and through the storm
Oh no, You never let go
In every high and every low
Oh no, You never let go
Lord, You never let go of me

from NEVER LET GO, *by Matt Redmon*

The crowd erupted in applause and tears! But it wasn't over yet. My friend Brian, the leader of the band, spoke up to say, "Matt, I heard you've been playing drums a little bit one handed."

"Ya, a little," I said.

He piped up with, "Get back there and jam a tune with us." I hesitated but then he of course had to ask the crowd, "Would you guys like to see Matt back at those drums?" And the crowd assured me that I needed to go for it.

As the band rolled into *"Won't Back Down"* by Tom Petty, I jumped in with a nice, solid, clean drum beat as the band sang:

"I'll stand my ground, won't be turned around. And I'll keep this world from dragging me down, gonna stand my ground... and I won't back down."

The energy erupted as we built up to a perfect rhythm and finished strong! Seven hundred people hit their feet and raised the roof in a standing ovation!

I could barely sleep that night. The mind pictures of all the moments of the evening flipped through my mind. I had done 'something' that night that brought me a fulfillment I had never encountered. Tom from 509 Films made the trip down to film the event for me. I just watched the footage today before writing this section, and it brought tears to my eyes and warmth to my heart.

Walk or Sink

Today, my neurological setback plagues me tremendously. I coach myself often to "practice what I speak" and challenge myself to monitor my PMA. I smile sometimes when I continue to ask myself, "How's your PMA?" But a positive attitude is literally the air in my raft, and if the air leaks out, I start to sink. I discipline myself to stay positive after a fall, or when my hand is too weak to open a bottle or jar, or when I'm unable to play with my boys in the manner that I would like.

I'm not working with what it could be, I'm working with what it is. I could try to wish it better, but if I don't participate, nothing will happen. I've been guilty of this, and I'm sure you have said too: "God just didn't answer my prayer. I prayed but nothing happened."

Let me challenge you with this: did you make yourself available to have that prayer answered? Did you do your part? Sure, sometimes we'll need to wait on the Lord, but at some point he'll require our participation. Placing the first foot forward is the first move required to walk in faith.

At one point, I cried out to God, "I want my life back. God, if you give me the strength, I'll do *whatever* it takes." The Bible doesn't say that Jesus floated Peter across the water to Him. It says that Peter walked on water to get out to Him. Jesus asked Peter to participate; to put one foot in front of the other and in Faith, walk across the water.

I played no role in surviving the beating that my body sustained. It is a miracle, plain and simple. But once I was out of my coma, God gave me the strength to walk on water, but he didn't float or carry me, he challenged me to do my part, to put one foot in front of the other, learn something with every step, and we're still walking. Sometimes the waves toss and roar a bit, but He promises that if I never take my eyes off of Him, I'll never sink.

Build Something Beautiful

I've been asked a few times if I think I should wait until my recovery is complete before I write a book. The reality that I've had to accept is that I won't cross the finish line in my recovery until I step into heaven. Recovery is and will be my way of life, for life. But I'm still living! I make the choice to *live* through my struggles, not just survive through them.

I'm amazed how what appeared to be a complete disaster has presented so much opportunity. My God inspired response to adversity allowed me to see it clearly. On the flip side, a negative reaction could have fogged the horizon to see only stress and struggle in the future. A friend sent me an encouraging quote in the thick of my recovery; "We are all faced with a series of great opportunities brilliantly disguised as impossible situations" (UNKNOWN). I faced something that was nearly impossible to recover from.

Faith and hope were my pry bars to use "nearly" as a door to pry on and eventually to break through. As I flipped through the pages of THE POWER TO PREVAIL, I read and believed that *"With God's help, you can build something beautiful out of the ashes of any adversity."* I see beauty within arm's reach, on the horizon, and beauty in the next generation as my Potratz boys become young men. I

> *When it is my time, and I stand at the gates of heaven, I hope that I have no time, talent, or resources left to give, nothing held back.*

couldn't clean up these ashes, it seemed impossible to recover from adversity of this magnitude. But, I raised my ashes to heaven with one weak hand, and God turned them into beauty; into a new morning.

I very nearly took an early trip to heaven and quite honestly, there were a lot of pieces of the puzzle that I had neglected to place where they belong. I would have stood before God apologizing and explaining why. When it is my time, and I stand at the gates of heaven, I hope that I have no time, talent, or resources left to give; nothing held back, and I can say: I took everything You gave me, and found a way to give it away. *I made my mark!*

– 12 –
WEARING A NEW PASSION

"A river flows smoothly only after a lifetime of passion and purpose."

Unknown

I RECENTLY READ A QUOTE THAT'S BECOME MY FAVORITE SIX WORDS; "LIVE YOUR DREAM, WEAR YOUR PASSION." I've been accused many times of dreaming too big, even of wasting my time because, "it's just not realistic." My question is always, "Realistic by whose standards?" By many standards, it's not realistic for me to be an author today, but I am! I'm proud to be one that views life differently and it's an honor to lead others to do so with me.

Bobby Kennedy said many times, *"Some men see things as they are and say 'Why?' I dream things that never were, and say 'Why not?'"* Dreams change as life changes. My dreams were interrupted by something we all dread. I learned to dream a new dream in the midst of my dreads. My dreads took my attention temporarily but I starved my dreads of energy they could soak up in order to feed my new dreams.

I have always worn my emotions and feelings, and my passion, like a logo on the front of my shirt. Whatever I'm involved in, if I'm passionate about it, you know it. I was passionate about a handful of things, but for sure snowmobiling. I often referred to it as "my

> *I learned to dream a new dream in the midst of my dreads.*

passion" and still do today. The one thing I had lost passion for was the only thing that matters to be passionate about; a relationship with Jesus Christ.

I've had a handful of friends ask me, "So what's this God thing all about? Why is there a Jesus and a God? Why does it matter so much to you?" You might be wondering the same thing. It's really quite simple. I'm sure you agree that none of us are perfect and this crazy world we live in is far from perfect. God on the other hand, *is* perfect. He always has been and always will be. When he created humans, we were perfect in his eyes. In fact the Bible even says that we are "created in His likeness." So yes, that means we look like God. Not nearly as glorious and beautiful, but we are the most complex and beautiful creatures on this earth because we are "like" our Creator.

When He placed us perfect on this earth, His rules in the Garden of Eden were simple; don't eat the forbidden fruit—just one fruit, you can eat all the rest. It's kind of like we tell our kids, "Don't eat the yellow snow." Pretty simple, right? But it wasn't. It just felt so right because we might be missing out on the most delicious fruit in the garden.

What felt so perfect ended up being mankind's first imperfection. So we are not perfect in God's eyes, we continued to sin from that point forward. But here's the good news; though not perfect, we are *accepted* in God's eyes. He created us in His likeness! With Him, we work from approval, not for approval. I'm going to say that again: with God, you work *from* approval, not for approval. No extra special work you can do will make him love you more. You're accepted, you're approved! You can get closer to him, but He can't love you more because His love for you is already off the charts!

But because we are not perfect and God is perfect, we couldn't really access God. We put up that barrier of imperfection when we sinned. Over time, it broke God's heart as the world became plagued by sin and corruption. Back in that day, it was common to make real, live sacrifices to God of sheep, goats, lamb, and others. Valuable livestock was burnt over open flame as a sacrifice to God. That's where Jesus comes in; to fill the gap for our imperfection, God offered His own son to stand in that gap, to hang on a cross and die as the ultimate *sacrifice* once and for all.

The best part is that He first sent Jesus into our world to be born as a baby, grow up as a boy, and to live as a man. He experienced our world exactly the way that we experience it; the same pain, the same stress, the same struggles, the same highs and the same lows.

He humbled himself to be a man while on this earth. Paul shares in Philippians that although he was God, He didn't walk through our world as God. He felt it the way that we feel it:

> "Though he was God, he did not think of equality with God as something to cling to. Instead, he gave up his divine privileges; he took the humble position of a slave and was born as a human being. When he appeared in human form, he humbled himself in obedience to God and died a criminal's death on a cross." Philippians 2:6-8(NLT).

Through Jesus, we can access God. His life sacrificed has been and always will be enough for us to have a real, vibrant relationship with our Creator, regardless of our imperfections. Jesus put Heaven in touch with Earth. When you pray, when you cry, when you laugh, when you hurt, He gets it. He lived it! He suffered human pain when they mocked him, beat him, whipped him and drove big metal spikes through his hands that hung him on a wooden cross to die that painful death.

The Glue Of Life

Maybe you're one of my fans or readers and you're just not sure about all this "God stuff." That's totally understandable. At times I've been turned off by all the "God stuff" and maybe you have too. There was even a time in my life when I walked away from it all. I was so tired of *religion*. Then I felt a void in my life that I could not fill. I'm sure you know the feeling I'm talking about.

I'm learning that God is very interested in *relationship* and could care less about religion. People have said to me, "Now your religious, right?" My reply to that is, "Nope, not religious, I'm relational." It's as simple as loving God, and loving people. Nothing more, nothing less. I believe that quality of life can be narrowed down to one word; Love. Merriam Webster

> *At times, I've been turned off by all the "God stuff," and maybe you have too.*

classifies love as a noun and the definition you'll find is this: "*strong affection for another arising out of kinship or personal ties (maternal love for a child) (2) : attraction based on sexual desire : affection and tenderness felt by lovers (3) : affection based on admiration, benevolence, or common interests.*" Sounds complicated to me. Love is more practical than that, and love also runs deeper than that. I view love as a *verb*, not a *noun*. It's something you *do*. Take a look at the bible's definition of *Love:*

> Love is patient, Love is kind, Love does not envy, Love does not boast, Love is not proud. It does not dishonor others, it is not self-seeking, it is not easily angered, it keeps no record of wrongs. Love does not delight in evil but rejoices with the truth. It always protects, always trusts, always hopes, always perseveres. 1 Corinthians 13: 4-7 (NIV)

That inspires action! Look back at those words again! Act out patience. Make every move in kindness. Discipline yourself to not envy, to not boast. Bury your pride. Keep no record of wrongs. Protect, trust, hope, persevere! Think of love as an action and act it out in every aspect of your life. When Jesus was cornered by the prideful religious clowns and asked "Which is the most important commandment?," He replied:

> 'You must love the Lord your God with all your heart, all your soul, and all your mind.' This is the first and greatest commandment. A second is equally important: 'Love your neighbor as yourself.' The entire law and all the

Without a doubt, this is why we ride. God hand-sculpted it all just for us. You might say, "Wow, I love this photo!" Well, the One who created this scene loves you back!

demands of the prophets are based on these two commandments." Matthew 22:37-40 (NLT)

With that phrase, Jesus laced it up tight! God *is* Love. God *commands* Love. If you learn to LOVE well, I can assure you that you'll live a truly fulfilled life. I loved well and it paid off. People came out from every side of life to love me through my crisis. I hadn't looked in quite some time, but as I write tonight, I found that the *Matt Potratz* page on the Caring Bridge website ended up at 34,812 visits from family and friends and I printed nearly 300 pages of encouraging comments. 35,000 times they said, "We love you enough to stand by you until this fight comes to an end."

There's no list of rules to follow in life, just *love well* and the rest will take care of itself. Friend, the best way to get what you want out of life is to give God what He wants in your life; His definition of Love.

What "Feels" Right

Often in life we go for what *feels* right, and many times end up missing what we *know* is right. Even if the right path is narrow, don't be afraid to veer out of your comfort zone. That path may not feel warm and fuzzy but it might be the only one that will allow you to complete your journey. Let's be real, life is not always going to feel warm and fuzzy. Adversity or struggle is part of life.

We don't serve a God who "makes" things happen to us. But, He "allows" things to happen to us. He allows us the freedom of choice to be the human race that had its beginning when Adam and Eve decided to taste the delicious forbidden fruit. That one fruit tree in the entire garden just "felt" so right.

Sometimes, that freedom of choice gets us in trouble. We're fortunate that we have a God who loves us enough to use all those "just too tasty" moments to mold us and shape us into who we are and make us stronger. We are not very moldable or shapeable when everything "feels" right. True change comes when we have to learn to choose the right path under fire.

A New Perspective

The great Arthur Ashe inspired this thought: I've at times said, "Why me, God? Why? Why did all of this have to happen to me?" Matt was on top; on a snowmobile, at work, a proud father, a musician, healthy, athletic. An avalanche stripped it all away and tumbled it off the mountain. I have to ask myself

> *"God, it's all yours— oh, except the snowmobile. That's my sport, my getaway, so that's something You should let me hang on to."*

now: did I ask, "Why me?" when I was one of the top riders in the nation and so blessed in nearly every aspect of life? All of that blessing was as much a part of his plan as allowing the avalanche to happen. Did I cry out to God, "Why me?" when life was so good?

Although it's very challenging to do, I've tried to model my perspective after Job in the bible. If you read the book of Job, you'll read about a man who faced tremendous adversity. He literally lost everything that he had in life except his very life. In his shattered and broken state, he wrote these words in Job 1:21:

> *"I came naked from my mother's womb, and I shall have nothing when I die.*
> *The Lord gave me everything that I had, and they were His to take away."*

I believe that it's okay to question God and at times even cry out to him in frustration. Broken and humble is right where God wants us to be and our cries for mercy can even be better than a hallelujah sometimes.

You might ask, why "broken?" Why would God put us through the feeling of brokenness? God doesn't desire to hurt us, to break us, but when we have tried

---

Speaking in Revelstoke, British Columbia

to face adversity in our own strength, our own way, and failed, we find ourselves broken. At that moment, we let go and let God steer the ship, which is right where He needs to be in this voyage we call life.

To "let go, and let God" can be so difficult but so rewarding. The word in Job's writing that I've found to be difficult to tackle is the word "everything." *"The Lord gave me 'everything' that I had, and they were his to take away."*

We tend to say, "Okay God, you have my house, my car, my money, even my family. I'll lay it all down when you need my time. God, it's all yours—oh, except the snowmobile. That's my sport, my getaway, so that's something You should let me hang on to. It's a priority for me. It helps me deal with the stress in life. It makes my long hours at work worth it," blah, blah, blah, right?

Maybe in your life it's not snowmobiling but most likely there's that little something that you hold dear. The verse doesn't say "everything, except," it simply says, "everything." Imagine the transformation in our lives and relationship with God if we would surrender ALL and truly place everything that we have in His hands. I promise you this: He'll do a better job with it, and He'll definitely ask us to actively participate.

God's probably not going to ask you to park the boat, the snowmobile, quit the golf club, leave the girlfriend, have less for your family, whatever it may be. Surrender just means not allowing it to rule your life. It's willingness to seek His direction in every move that we make in this life.

I'm sure that if you're a parent, you're like me and want to give your family the best quality of life you can offer; making sure there's food on the table, money for family needs, comfort, education, even fun. That desire is perfect! In fact, I believe God honors that.

As always, the Bible laces the shoes of this subject up nice and tight. In Matthew 6:32, Jesus says, *"For your heavenly Father knows that you need all these things."* He shares your same desire to see your family's needs met! The rubber meets the road in verse 33 when He goes on to say, *"But seek first the kingdom of God and His righteousness, and all these things shall be added to you" (NIV).* The New Living Translation text ends with *"and He will give you everything you need."* Not much more to say. Seek Him FIRST, and ALL your needs will be met.

A New Man

When I lost my job, yet drove away in peace, I didn't know why. But God has slowly unwrapped the gift of a new life, lived by a new man. As an author, speaker, and life coach, I often refer to myself as a full-time "investor." I'm finding out exactly why I walked away from my career crushed and confused, yet had that deep down calming peace: I had already placed my life in God's hands. He was steering the ship. That peace was my faith that He had a plan. He was going to show me a new kind of "investment."

I am discovering a compensation and reward that far exceeds the largest paycheck I've ever received. It's the best investment I have ever made but has nothing to do with money. I'm investing in lives, in people.

It felt great to be successful by our busy world's standards; to have a title, to have authority, to bring home a healthy paycheck. But it was truly not even comparable to the reward of looking out across a crowd of young people passing tissue to dry their tears as my story and message has touched their lives.

I would lay down my pressed shirt and title to be daddy and get my shirt dirty with my boys more often. I would burn a big paycheck to find the fulfillment of lunch with a young man in a wheelchair that finds connection with my crisis and hope in my story and positive attitude.

Three hearts and six more hands will reach out and touch their world.

My resume full of education and work experience means nothing to the men I meet with weekly who are battling through drug or alcohol addiction rehabilitation. However, my response to adversity means *everything* to them. They feed off of my friendship, positive energy, and my example.

If I was the successful sales manager, professional snowmobiler—the guy who had it made, I wouldn't have a platform to stand on to touch young lives, help people rehabilitate, or to invest in those struggling in life. But, because I've stared adversity in the face, turned my eyes to Heaven for strength, and chosen to respond, not react, they feel a true connection. They tell me that I "get it," that I know what they're going through. Their hearts are open, so when I reach out my hand, they latch on tight.

With Two Hands, we go from crawling to coasting to climbing and become victors! With Two Hands, my boys hold tight to daddy's hand as I guide their footsteps. Together, we all find that although falling down is a part of life,

getting back up and moving forward is living!

Works Cited

"2008 Avalanche Statistics," U.S. Census Bureau. Not currently available online. Formerly at http://www.census.gov/compendia/statab/2011/tables/11s1103

"Avalanche: Measurement, US Deaths, and Resources," T. Price, The Free Resource. Available online at http://www.thefreeresource.com/avalanche-measurement-us-deaths-and-resources

"God Gave Me You," by DAVE BARNES. Available on the album WHAT WE WANT, WHAT WE GET, released April 6, 2010. Copyright © 2010 Songs of Razor and Tie Obo No Gang Music Publishing.

"I Won't Back Down," by TOM PETTY & THE HEARTBREAKERS. Available on the album TOM PETTY & THE HEARTBREAKERS: GREATEST HITS, released March 9, 2010. Copyright © 2010 Geffen Records.

"I Won't Let Go," by RASCAL FLATTS. Available on the album NOTHING LIKE THIS, released November 16, 2010. Copyright © 2010 Big Machine Records, LLC.

"Once Again," by MATT REDMAN. Available on the album MATT REDMAN: ULTIMATE COLLECTION, released April 20, 2010. Copyright © 2010 Survivor Records Under Exclusive License to EMI Christian Music Group.

"Praise You In This Storm," by CASTING CROWNS. Available on the album LIFESONG, released August 30, 2005. Copyright © 2005 by Reunion Records.

"You Are More," by TENTH AVENUE NORTH. Available on the album THE LIGHT MEETS THE DARK, released May 11, 2010. Copyright © 2010 Provident Label Group LLC, a unit of Sony Music Entertainment.

"You Never Let Go," by MATT REDMAN. Available on the album MATT REDMAN: ULTIMATE COLLECTION, released April 20, 2010. Copyright © 2010 Survivor Records Under Exclusive License to EMI Christian Music Group.

Firewind PRODUCTIONS

design, consulting, new media, and websites that start wildfires

You bring
the *fuel*,
we'll bring
the *fire*

IF YOU HAVE PASSION AND A PURPOSE, we can help you take your big ideas to the next level—both on and off the web. We specialize in *idea ignition* via new and traditional media, custom website design, consulting, and a full range of design, illustration and publishing services. We're especially passionate about serving creatives, non-profits and ministries. Are you ready to change your world? *Let's go start a fire!*

FirewindProductions.com OFFICE/TEXT: 208.298.9083

Created...

...creating.